Fast Ideas for Busy Teachers

Math

Grade 2

by
Vicky Shiotsu

Illustrations by
Corbin Hillam

Published by Frank Schaffer Publications
an imprint of
McGraw Hill Children's Publishing

Author: Vicky Shiotsu
Editor: Cindy Barden

McGraw-Hill Children's Publishing

Published by Instructional Fair
An imprint of McGraw-Hill Children's Publishing

Send all inquiries to:
McGraw-Hill Children's Publishing
3195 Wilson Drive NW
Grand Rapids, Michigan 49544

Fast Ideas for Busy Teachers: Math—Grade 2
ISBN: 0-7682-2912-X

1 2 3 4 5 6 7 8 9 MAL 09 08 07 06 05 04
The McGraw-Hill Companies

Table of Contents

Introduction

Packed with hundreds of quick tips, fun ideas, and reproducibles, the *Fast Ideas for Busy Teachers: Math* series provides a wonderful resource designed to make a busy teacher's life easier. Ideas for stocking and organizing your math center, individual and group activities, games, reproducibles, patterns, puzzles, explorations of concepts, and much more invite students to learn about math through creative and fun hands-on activities.

Fast Ideas for Busy Teachers: Math supplements your math curriculum with warm-up or follow-up exercises, take-home pages, in-class assignments, and rainy-day activities to help students master a variety of mathematical concepts and skills. Organization by content related to various math skills makes it quick and easy to find the material you need, when you need it. A wide variety of open-ended material allows you to adapt activities to meet the specific needs of your class or individual students. Watch enthusiasm for math grow as students discover how valuable and fun learning math can be!

Teacher resource pages include organizational tips; suggestions for manipulatives; patterns; and a variety of individual, partner, and small group activities designed to increase students' understanding of math. Preparation time and supplies needed are minimal and include items normally available in classrooms.

Fast Ideas for Busy Teachers: Math topics and skill areas are based on the current NCTM Principles and Standards for School Mathematics, designed by the National Council of Teachers of Mathematics. They include number and operations; algebra; geometry; measurement; data analysis and probability skills through problem-solving strategies, reasoning and proof, mathematical connections, representations, and communications. For specific information, see the matrix showing the correlation of the activities and tips to the NCTM Standards.

Fast Ideas for Busy Teachers: Math allows you to plan creative, motivating activities and incorporate them in your math curriculum. Best of all, students' enthusiasm for math grows when math becomes an adventure of fun and discovery!

Meeting the NCTM Standards

Correlation Chart

	PROBLEM SOLVING	REASONING & PROOF	CONNECTIONS	REPRESENTATION	COMMUNICATION
NUMBER & OPERATIONS	7, 8, 9, 10, 11, 12, 13, 19, 20, 21, 22, 44, 47, 48, 49, 50, 51, 52, 53, 54, 55, 56, 57, 59, 60, 61, 62, 64, 65, 66, 67, 68, 79	13, 19, 32, 33, 34, 54, 55, 56, 57	9, 10, 11, 13, 21, 22, 48, 49, 51, 57, 59, 61, 62, 65, 68, 79	11, 12, 13, 14, 22, 32, 33, 44, 46, 49, 50, 51, 54, 55, 58, 63, 64, 79, 80	22, 34, 52, 59, 60, 61, 65, 66, 67
ALGEBRA	33, 46, 52	23, 32, 35, 46	23, 45	23, 45, 47	23, 35
GEOMETRY	24, 25, 26, 27	24, 25, 28, 29, 31	24, 25	25, 26, 27	24, 26, 28, 29, 30, 31
MEASUREMENT	36, 38, 39, 40, 41, 42, 43, 69, 72, 73, 74, 75	39, 40, 69, 70, 71, 72, 73, 75	37, 38, 39, 42, 43, 72, 73, 75	30, 37, 70, 73, 74	41, 69, 70, 73
DATA ANALYSIS & PROBABILITY	17, 18, 36, 70, 76, 77, 78	70, 76, 77, 78	15, 16, 17, 76, 78	15, 16, 17, 18, 36, 42, 76, 78	15, 16, 36, 70, 76, 78

Adding and Subtracting to 20

Number Sentence Workout

Reinforce computational skills with this quick activity. Write a number on the board and have students write as many number sentences as they can to equal that number. You can add restrictions to make the activity more challenging, such as using at least three numbers; using two-digit numbers; or using two operations in one number sentence.

Variety Is the Spice of Learning

Vary your math counters to keep student interest high. Milk jug caps, nature items (small shells, pebbles, large seeds), buttons, beads, and rubber bugs make terrific fun manipulatives for students.

Plus or Minus Race

Pair up students and give each pair a set of number cards from 1 to 20. Explain how to play this fast-paced game. Instruct each student to flip over two cards and mentally subtract the lesser number from the greater number. The first player to say the correct answer wins the cards. The game ends when one player wins all the cards. For an extra challenge, let students repeat the game, adding the numbers instead of subtracting.

Zigzag Math

On the board, write a "zigzag equation" made up of five addition and subtraction equations as shown below:

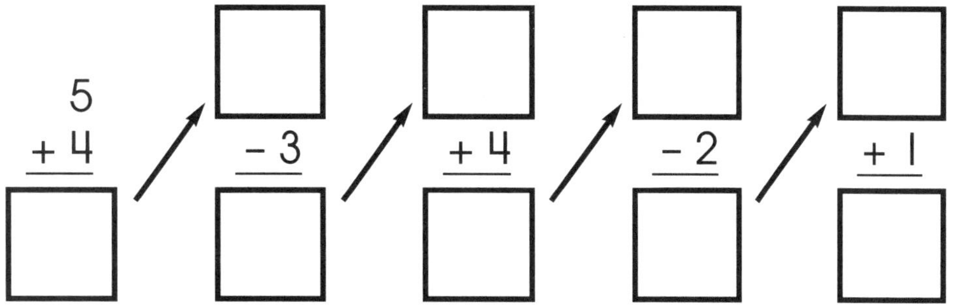

After students copy the equations on a sheet of paper, they can fill in the boxes. Be certain students notice that each answer becomes a part of the next equation. Call on student volunteers to fill in the boxes on the board.

For a follow-up activity, give each student a copy of "Zigzag Math." Challenge students to write their own sets of equations. Students can leave the boxes for the answers blank, then trade papers with a partner and complete each other's work.

Name ______________________________ Date ______________

Zigzag Math

Fill in the boxes for the first equation. Use the answer to your first equation to make your second equation. Keep going until you have filled in all of the boxes.

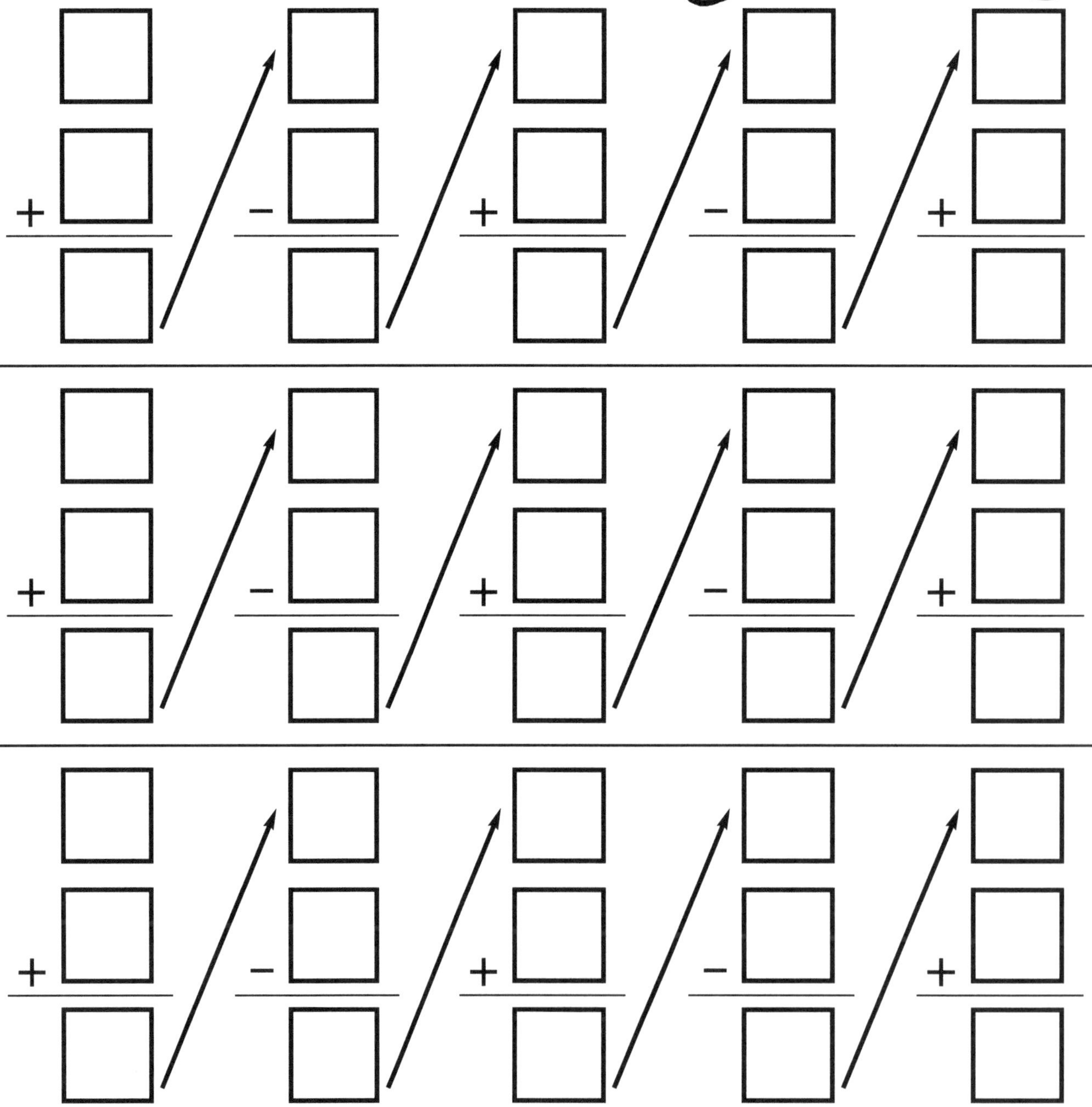

Adding and Subtracting to 20

Add the Letters

Reinforce computation with this combination math and spelling activity. Make a copy of "Add the Letters" for each student. Each of the ten letters has a point value. Students should make as many words as they can, using only the letters given.

Words must be worth at least nine points to count. If students have difficulty adding up the points mentally, encourage them to use counters or tally marks to calculate each word's score.

If desired, set a time limit. When they finish, students can share their words and point values with the class.

Silence Is Golden

To reduce the noise when the class is using manipulatives, have students place plastic or cloth place mats on their desks.

Math Facts Concentration

Add a fun twist to the traditional memory game. Cut out 32 4" x 6" pieces of cardstock. Attach the cards to a bulletin board, stapling around the sides and bottom edges to form pockets. Make four rows of four pockets on the left half of the board and a similar set of pockets on the right half. Position the pockets low enough so students can reach them easily. Title the left side "Equations" and the right side "Solutions."

Prepare 16 index cards (3" x 5") by writing a math equation on each one. Write corresponding answers on another set of 16 cards. Insert one card in each pocket.

Divide the class into two teams. Let each team take turns pulling an "equation" card and a "solution" card. If the cards match, the team keeps both cards. If the cards don't match, they return the cards to their original pockets. The game continues until teams match all of the cards. The team with the most cards wins.

Fact Traveling

In this action-packed activity, students "travel" around the room as they practice their math facts. Number 20 index cards and write an addition or subtraction equation on each card. Place the cards around the room (on countertops, tables, shelves, and so on).

Have students number the left-hand side of their papers from 1 to 20. At your signal, students move from card to card, copy the equations, and write the answers. Set a time limit, or continue the activity until all students have copied each equation. Afterwards, go over the answers with the class.

Name ______________________________ Date ______________

Add the Letters

Make words using letters from the chart. Words must be worth at least 9 points. Write your words and the points on the lines. See how many you can get!

A	E	I	O	U	M	S	P	T	B
0	1	2	3	4	5	6	7	8	9

Word	Points	Word	Points

Place Value to 100

Scoop and Count

Divide the class into small groups and give each group a paper plate, a container of 70 to100 small counters such as beans, buttons, bingo chips, or beads, and several three-inch paper squares for each student.

Students take turns scooping up some counters in one hand and placing them on the group's plate. Group members estimate how many counters are on the plate. Each student writes an estimate on a paper square and turns it facedown.

After the group determines the actual number of counters on the plate by making sets of tens and ones, students turn their paper squares faceup. The one with the closest estimate wins that round and collects one counter. Students should repeat the activity several times. The winner in each group is the student with the most counters.

Place Value Mats

Place value mats are helpful tools for teaching place value concepts. To make place value mats, glue two sheets of construction paper in contrasting colors to the inside of a file folder. Label the left half of the mat "Tens" and the right half "Ones." Use the mats with manipulatives such as craft sticks or linking cubes for a variety of place value activities.

Number Detective

Give each student a copy of the "100 Number Board" and a set of 20 counters. Tell students they are going to be "number detectives." As you give clues about numbers on the 100 Number Board, they find the matching numbers and cover them with the counters. Vary the clues depending on the abilities of your class.

This number has 4 tens and 8 ones. What is it? (48)

This number is between 72 and 79. It has a 5 in the ones place. What is it? (75)

This number is 3 tens more than 26. What is it? (56)

These odd numbers have 3 or 5 in the tens place. What are they?
(31, 33, 35, 37, 39, 51, 53, 55, 57, 59)

This is the highest even number on the chart that has the same digit in both the tens and ones places. What is it? (88)

Name ______________________ Date ____________

100 Number Board

1	2	3	4	5	6	7	8	9	10
11	12	13	14	15	16	17	18	19	20
21	22	23	24	25	26	27	28	29	30
31	32	33	34	35	36	37	38	39	40
41	42	43	44	45	46	47	48	49	50
51	52	53	54	55	56	57	58	59	60
61	62	63	64	65	66	67	68	69	70
71	72	73	74	75	76	77	78	79	80
81	82	83	84	85	86	87	88	89	90
91	92	93	94	95	96	97	98	99	100

Place Value to 100

Place Value Flip Books

Make two sets of "Number Cards" for each student. Copy one set on orange paper and the other set on yellow paper (or use other contrasting colors). Students will also need scissors, staplers, and cardstock. Explain how to make place value flipbooks:

1. Cut out the cards. Keep the two sets in separate piles. Arrange numbers in order with 0 on the top and 9 on the bottom.
2. Staple the top portion of one set of cards to the top left portion of a piece of cardstock. Staple the other set on the top right side.
3. At the bottom of the cardstock, write "Tens" on the left half and "Ones" on the right half.

Use the flip books for activities that reinforce place value and number identification. See suggestions below.

Name a number, such as 52. Students flip their cards to show the number.

Call out tens and ones, such as four tens and eight ones. Students flip their cards to show the matching number.

Give a clue, such as the number after 39. Students flip their cards to show the correct number.

Show Me

Students can use their place value flip books to create numbers based on various criteria. Here are some examples:

Show a number that is greater than 35 but less than 55.

Show a number with a ones digit greater than the tens digit.

Show a number with a ones digit three less than the tens digit.

Show an even number with two even-numbered digits.

Show an even number with one odd-numbered digit.

Number Cards

0	1	2
3	4	5
6	7	8
9		

Family Graph

This graphing activity provides an opportunity for students to create either vertical or horizontal bar graphs. Cut 3" paper squares from colored paper and 1 ½" circles from light brown paper. Explain to students that they will be making picture graphs of their families.

Students will need as many circles and squares as there are people in their families. Each circle represents one family member. Instruct them to glue each circle onto a square, draw facial features, and write the name of the family member.

Students should glue their squares onto 3" x 18" paper strips. The sides of the squares should touch. For a vertical graph, students glue the squares so the faces stack on top of one another. For a horizontal graph, students glue the squares so the faces are side by side. After the squares are glued in place, students trim the strips. If some students need longer strips, they can tape a second strip to the first one.

Finally, have the class tape their strips along the edge of a sheet of butcher paper. Have students study the graph to answer these questions:

> Who has the largest family?
>
> Who has the smallest family?
>
> How many students have more than five people in their family?
>
> How many students have only three people in their family?
>
> Which is greater—the number of students with four people in their family or the number of students with five people in their family?

Amazing Animals

Read *Biggest, Strongest, Fastest,* by Steve Jenkins, to the class. This colorful picture book provides information about animal record-holders: the biggest, strongest, fastest, etc. Use the book as a springboard for students to make their own comparisons of animals.

Let students work in pairs to research a particular feature either among different kinds of animals or in a specific animal group. One pair might compare the weights of a variety of animals, while another pair could research the lengths of various snakes. Afterwards, have students graph their information and share their displays with the class.

Graphing

Reading Graphs

Encourage students to keep track of how many minutes they spend each day reading for pleasure. Have students record their minutes on a sheet of paper. At the end of a week, students can graph the results on individual bar graphs. Ask:

On which day did you read the most?
On which day did you read the least?
How many minutes did you read on Monday and Tuesday?

For an extra challenge, make the reading graph an ongoing activity and set a daily or weekly goal for students. At the end of each week, award certificates or small prizes to those who reached their goals.

Quick Graphs

Keep a supply of one-inch graph paper on hand for students to create bar graphs. If graph paper isn't available, make a grid with a felt marker. Use the grid as a master for copying as needed.

Favorite Colors

This activity provides an easy way to introduce students to circle graphs. Divide the class into groups of six. Give each group two copies of the "Circle Graph Pattern" page. Have students cut one of the circles apart. Tell the class that each section represents a student.

Students use the wedge patterns to cut out same-size wedges from construction paper that match their favorite colors. Have students glue their wedges to the group's circle with same-color wedges placed next to each other. The result will be a circle graph displaying each group's color preferences.

Variation:

Students can use the "Circle Graph Pattern" to display other types of information, such as favorite ice cream flavors or favorite fruits. Use a different color of construction paper to represent each preference, such as red for strawberry, yellow for banana, and so on.

Add and Graph

Combine adding and graphing with this activity. Give each student two dice, a copy of "Add and Graph," and a crayon or colored pencil. Tell students to roll the dice, total the two numbers, and graph the total. Have them repeat this process 11 more times. Divide students into pairs to discuss their graphs. Suggest questions to get them started:

Which sum came up most often?
What sum was rolled in Roll 6?
What was the largest sum?
How many times did you get a sum of 5?

Have pairs list their questions and their findings on a sheet of paper. Post the papers on a bulletin board so students can compare the different results.

Circle Graph Pattern

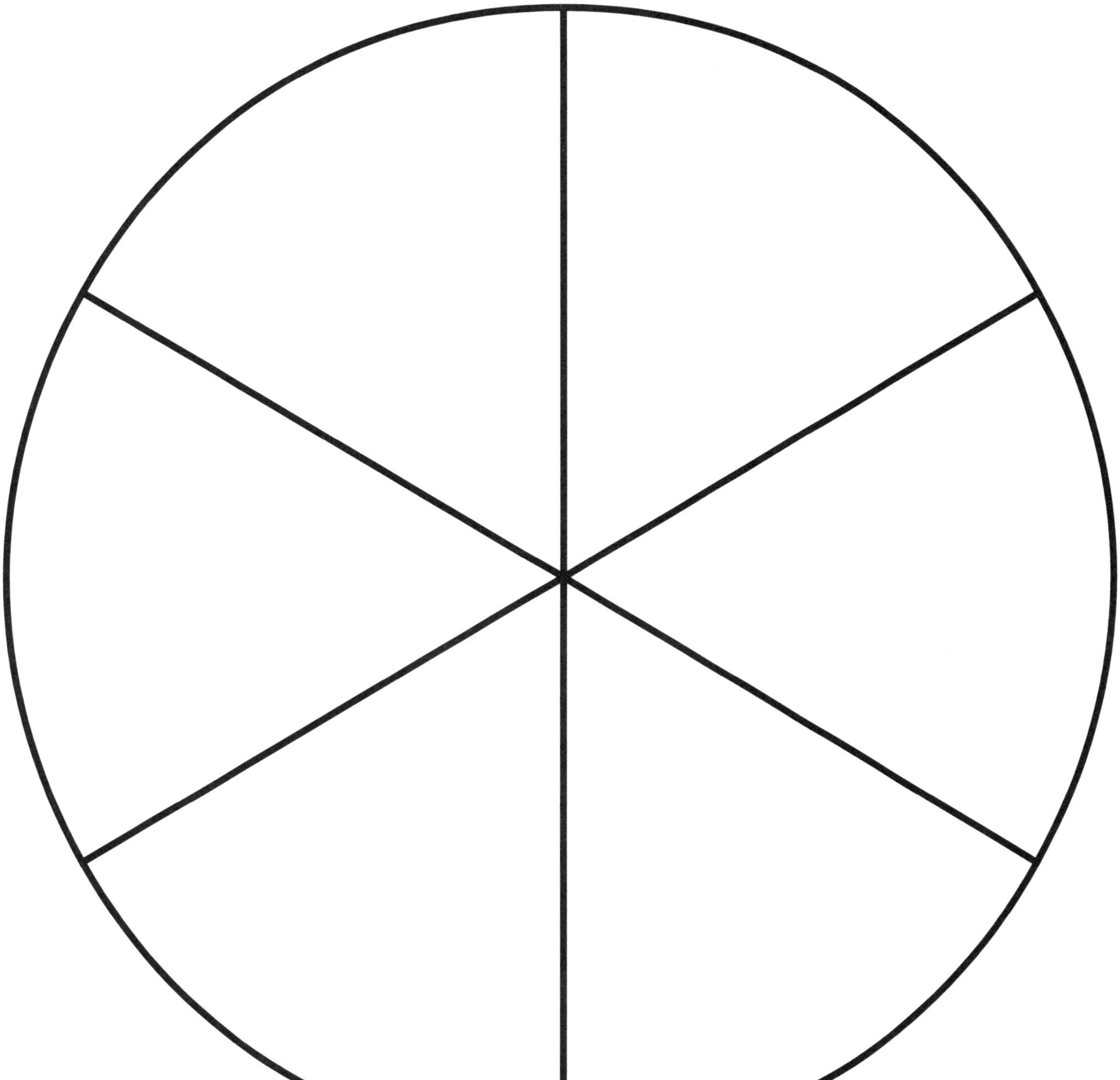

Name ______________________________ Date ______________

Add and Graph

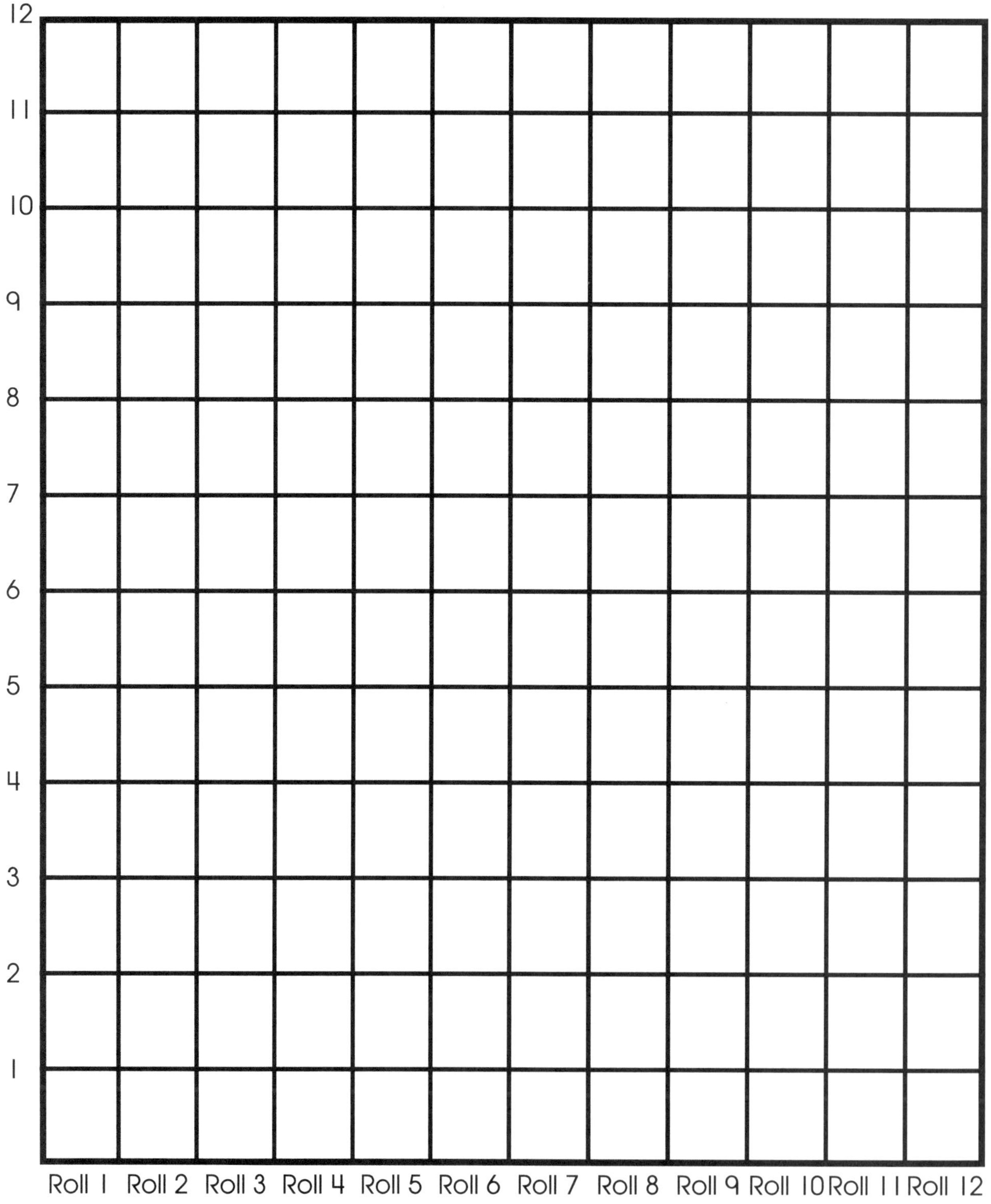

Adding and Subtracting Two-Digit Numbers

Mental Math Tips

Give each student a copy of the "100 Number Board" to demonstrate a quick way to add mentally. Write 27 + 9 on the board. Have students find 27 on the chart. Demonstrate to students how to find the answer to 27 + 10 by looking at the number in the next row directly under the 27 (37).

Show them that to add 9, they can add 10 and then subtract 1 to get 36. Repeat with other examples, such as 45 + 9 and 68 + 9.

Repeat the activity to show how to add 19 quickly (add 20 and subtract 1). Extend the learning by having students determine quick tricks for adding 29, 39, and so on.

Encourage Self-Checking

When students complete subtraction equations, encourage them to check their work by addition. For example, if students write that 83 minus 25 equals 68, then they should add 68 and 25 to see that they do not get 83. Checking subtraction by addition not only reinforces the concept of inverse relationships, but also promotes self-checking and accuracy.

Mystery Equations

Students manipulate numbers to create their own equations in this activity. Make two copies of the "Number Cards" page, cut the cards apart, and put them in a lunch bag. Make a copy of "Mystery Equations" for each student. If you want students to do only addition equations or only subtraction equations, cut the pages in half and give them the appropriate half.

Next, draw a number card from the bag, call out the number, and have each student write it in a box of his choice for the first equation. Repeat the procedure two more times, as students fill in the remaining boxes of the first equation.

Return the number cards to the bag, shake the bag to mix up the cards, and repeat the activity for the rest of the equations on the sheet. Have student solve the equations. If a student creates a subtraction equation in which the bottom number is greater than the top number, have him switch the places of the tens digits.

When they finish, ask students to write their equations and solutions on the board.

Name ______________________________ Date ______________

Mystery Equations

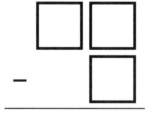

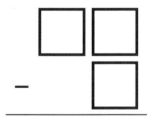

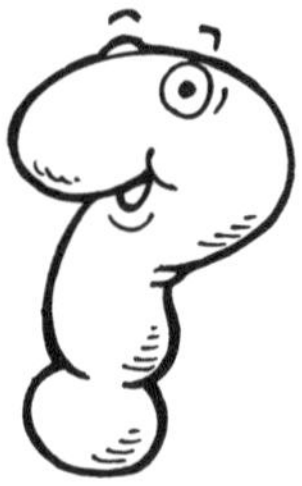

Addition:

□□ + □		□□ + □		□□ + □	
□□ + □□		□□ + □□		□□ + □□	

Subtraction:

□□ − □		□□ − □		□□ − □	
□□ − □□		□□ − □□		□□ − □□	

Adding and Subtracting Two-Digit Numbers

Scavenge for Points

Prepare a list of small objects that can be found on your school grounds and assign a value to each item. See sample below. Pair up students. Give each pair a small plastic bag and the list of items.

Tell students they need to find enough items from the list to reach a certain number of points, such as 75. Be sure the value you give can be met by more than one combination of objects. Send the class off on a 15-minute scavenger hunt.

At the end of the hunt, pairs return to the classroom and tally the value of their objects. If they are over or under the number of points needed to win, have them decide what to take away from or add to their collection to achieve the exact number of points. Let students trade items with other pairs.

rock – 15 points
blade of grass – 5 points
twig – 10 points
leaf – 10 points
leaf longer than 4 inches – 15 points
all-white rock – 20 points

Folktale Math

Read Walter Dean Meyers' *How Mr. Monkey Saw the Whole World* to the class. This delightful folktale tells how Mr. Buzzard tricks animals into giving him food. Mr. Monkey sees the other animals being cheated and decides to teach Mr. Buzzard a lesson.

After reading the book, let students make up addition and subtraction equations based on the story. Have students write their equations on index cards and add illustrations. Place the cards at a learning center where students can work on the equations in small groups.

Family Sums Challenge

Have each student estimate the sum of the ages of her family members and list the estimates on a sheet of chart paper. That night, have students work out the actual sums at home with the help of their families. The next day, students can write the actual sums beside their estimates to see who had the most accurate estimate.

Extend the activity by asking students to calculate what the sums would be if they were based on ages one year later, five years later, two years earlier, etc.

100 Number Board Patterns

Note: Each student will need a copy of the "100 Number Board" page for these activities.

What's Missing?

Give each student a handful of small counters. Write a pattern with a missing number on the board, such as 3, 6, 9, 12, __, 18, 21. Have students place counters on the corresponding numbers on their 100 Number Boards. Ask students to describe the pattern and determine the missing number. Continue with other patterns. Here are some examples:

5, 10, 15, ___, 20, ____ (Count by fives.)
1, 3, 5, 7, 9, ___ (Start with 1 and add 2.)
1, 6, 11, 16, 21, ___ (Start with 1 and add 5.)
10, 21, 32, 43, ___ (Start with 10 and add 11.)

Extension Activity:

Let students write their own patterns on the board and challenge classmates to find the missing numbers.

Reusable 100 Number Boards

A 100 Number Board is a valuable tool for helping students see number patterns. Bingo chips and paper squares are ideal counters for the 100 Number Board. To make reusable boards, laminate them or place them inside plastic sheet protectors and seal with cellophane tape.

Mystery Patterns

Students select a number pattern and color the squares on their 100 Number Boards according to that pattern. Ask each student to write the rule for the pattern on an index card. Display the 100 Number Boards and the rules on a bulletin board. Discuss the patterns with the class.

Ask: Which patterns made a diagonal design on the chart? (Patterns that involve counting by 3, 9, and 11 will form diagonal designs.)

Which patterns made a vertical design on the chart? (Patterns that involve counting by 2, 5, or 10 will form vertical designs.)

Did any patterns create two vertical rows? (Patterns that involve counting by 5 will form two vertical rows.)

Gues-s-s My Pattern

Give each student a copy of "Gues-s-s My Pattern." When they complete the activity, display the snakes on a bulletin board. Have groups of students take turns going to the board, studying the numbers, and finding the patterns.

Name ______________________________ Date ______________

Gues-s-s My Pattern

Place counters on a 100 Number Board to create a number pattern.

Write the numbers you covered on the snake.

On the back of the page, write the pattern's rule.

Plane Figures

Shape Posters

Divide the class into small groups and provide each group with butcher paper and magazines. Students can cut out pictures of objects with geometric shapes–tires, crackers, windows, and so on. Instruct each group to sort the pictures according to their shapes and glue them onto the butcher paper to make a poster.

Each group can make a bar graph showing how many pictures of each shape they found. Display the posters and bar graphs on the wall. Students can study the graphs to determine which shape appeared most frequently and which one appeared the least.

Trace the Shapes

Collect relatively flat objects with distinct geometric shapes. Items can include plastic lids, small boxes, wooden blocks, cookie cutters, pattern blocks, and cardboard cutouts. Keep the objects in your math center for students to trace the shapes and make interesting geometric pictures and patterns.

Exploring Sides and Corners

Divide students into pairs and give each pair a copy of "Make Flat Shapes" and a plastic bag containing 12 cotton swabs. When students complete the activity, discuss the questions with the class. Ask some students to re-create their shapes with the swabs for the class. Guide students into understanding that the number of sides of a flat shape equals the number of corners.

Split Shapes

Here's a fun way to show students how to make different shapes from other shapes. Give students six-inch squares of colored paper and have them draw a line to split their square in half. Ask what shapes they created (two rectangles or two triangles). After students cut along their lines, have them glue the squares onto white paper, leaving a bit of space between the two pieces.

Repeat the activity with a rectangle and a triangle. Discuss the new shapes they created. (A rectangle will split into two triangles or two rectangles; a triangle will split into two triangles.)

For an extra challenge, have students draw two straight lines to split a square, a rectangle, and a triangle. Discuss the results. (Shapes will be quite varied. Two lines can split a square into three rectangles, four squares, or three triangles.) Have students glue the shapes onto white paper, leaving a thin space between the pieces.

Name ____________________ Date ____________

Make Flat Shapes

Use 12 cotton swabs. Write the answers.

1. Make a square.
   How many swabs did you use?______
   How many sides and corners does your square have?______

2. Make a triangle.
   How many swabs did you use?______
   How many sides and corners does your triangle have?______

3. Make a rectangle.
   How many swabs did you use?______
   How many sides and corners does your rectangle have?______

4. Make a different rectangle.
   How many swabs did you use? ______
   How many sides and corners does your rectangle have?_____

5. Use 12 swabs. Make an interesting shape with it. Draw the shape in the box.

   How many sides and corners does your shape have? ______

What did you learn about the number of sides and corners of flat shapes?

____

____

Plane Figures

Tangram Explorations

Grandfather Tang's Story by Ann Tompert is a delightful tale in which a Chinese grandfather uses tangrams to tell a folktale to his granddaughter. Read the story to the class. Make a copy of "A Tangram" for each student. (Reproducing the page on cardstock will make the tangram pieces sturdier.)

Have students identify the shapes of the seven pieces that make up the tangram. Then instruct students to cut out the pieces and arrange the shapes to make the animals shown. Follow up by challenging students to create their own tangram pictures or designs.

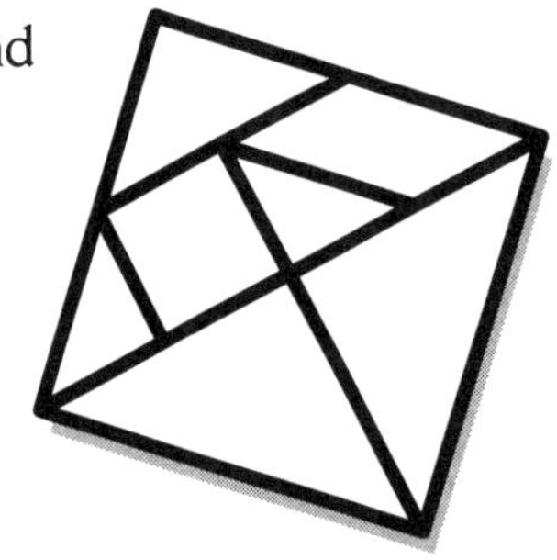

Grandfather Tang's Shapes

Store extra sets of tangrams in your math center along with a copy of the book *Grandfather Tang's Story* by Ann Tompert. When students have free time, encourage them to use the tangram pieces to make the pictures shown in the book and create their own shapes with tangrams.

Tangram Cover-Ups

Choose two or three tangram pieces and arrange them on a sheet of paper. Trace around the pieces to create a new shape. Repeat this procedure to make several shapes on the paper. Number the shapes and make a copy for each student.

As a group, have students use their tangram pieces from the last activity to determine which tangram pieces you used to make each shape.

Extension: Students can choose two or three tangram pieces and trace around them to create new shapes. Pair up students and have them determine which pieces their partners used.

Shapely Art

Show the class examples of paintings and collages that feature geometric shapes, such as the works of the Dutch painter Piet Mondrian. (Use a search engine to find examples on the Internet.)

Students can make their own designs using geometric shapes. Provide stencils or objects for tracing and let students cut shapes from colored paper or tissue paper. Remind them to arrange the shapes onto background paper first before gluing them in place. If they like, students can also use markers to draw additional shapes on their papers. Display the designs for the class to enjoy.

Name ______________________________ Date ______________

A Tangram

A tangram is a Chinese puzzle made from a square cut into seven pieces—five triangles, a square, and a parallelogram. The pieces are fitted together to make pictures. The pieces must touch, but cannot overlap.

Use the tangram pieces to make the fox, cat, and swan. Then make more pictures of your own.

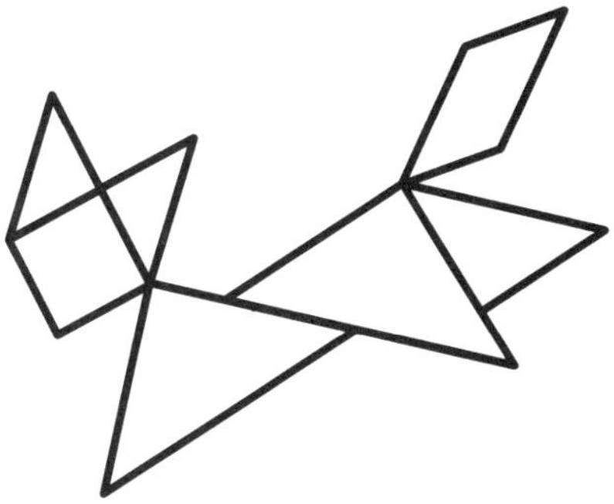

fox

swan

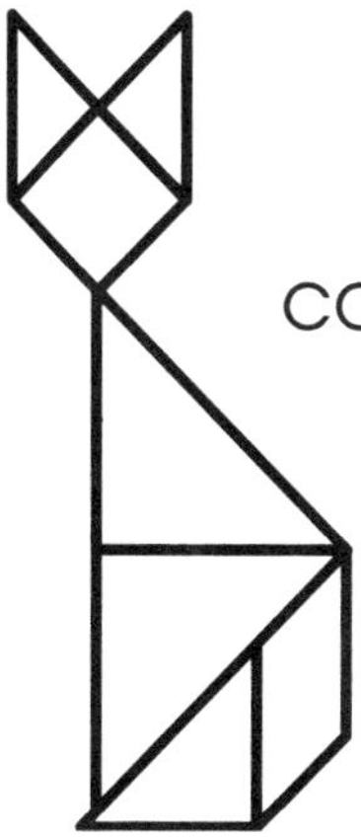

cat

1. Cut out the large square. Glue it onto black paper.
2. Cut along the lines to make seven pieces.
3. Turn the pieces over and work with the black side of each shape.

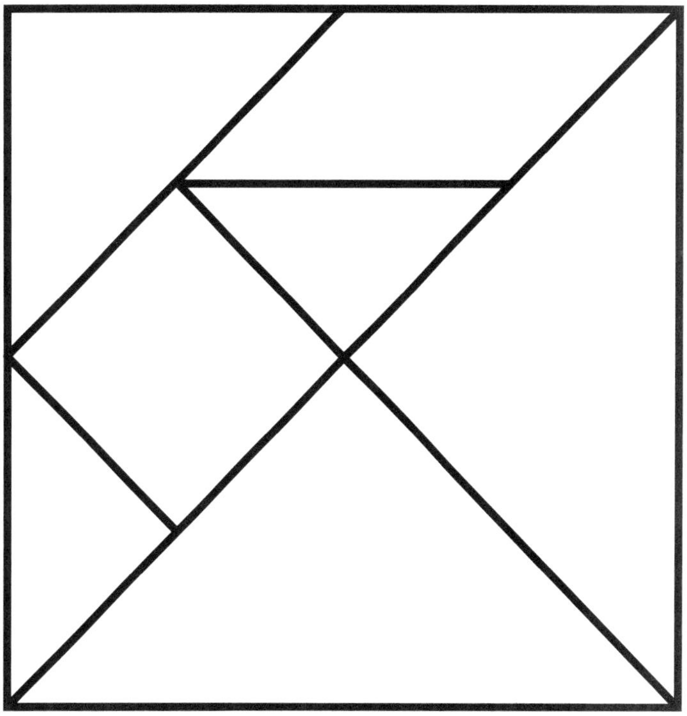

0-7682-2912-X *Fast Ideas for Busy Teachers: Math*

Geometric Solids

Geometric Scavenger Hunt

Send students on a geometric scavenger hunt to find geometric solids in your classroom, library, or gym. Provide a list of questions (see examples) to help them locate specific shapes.

What is in the cylinder on the third shelf of the supply cupboard?

What is in the rectangular box on the top of the teacher's desk?

Where is a sphere located in the classroom?

Who has a cone-shaped object on her desk?

Divide the class into teams and give each team a copy of the questions. The first team to answer all the questions correctly wins the hunt.

Request Contributions

Set up an area in the math center where students can study and compare geometric solids on their own. Ask parents to contribute geometric objects from home—balls, boxes, oatmeal canisters, lipstick tubes, toy blocks, short dowels, etc. Use the objects for a variety of classification and building activities.

Solids and Faces

Divide the class into small groups. Give each group a copy of "Solids and Faces" and a collection of solids. Hold up a solid and point to one of its flat sides. Have students notice that the flat side is shaped like a plane figure. Explain that the flat sides of solids are called "faces."

The faces should be drawn and labeled as follows: 1. cube—square; 2. cylinder—circle; 3. cone—circle; 4. rectangular prism—rectangle or square.

Discuss the findings with students. Then have them help you make a chart listing the different solids, the shapes of their faces, and the number of faces for each solid. Provide students with many examples of solids so they can see whether their findings hold true for all solids of a particular group.

Ask questions to help students form generalizations about solids and faces.

What shape is the face of a cylinder? (circle)

Do cylinders always have circular faces? (yes)

How many faces does a rectangular prism have? (6)

Do rectangular prisms always have faces shaped like rectangles? (No; some rectangular prisms may have faces shaped like squares.)

Name ______________________ Date ____________

Solids and Faces

Find a solid to match each picture. Trace around the face of each solid. Write the names of the shapes you drew.

1. Cube

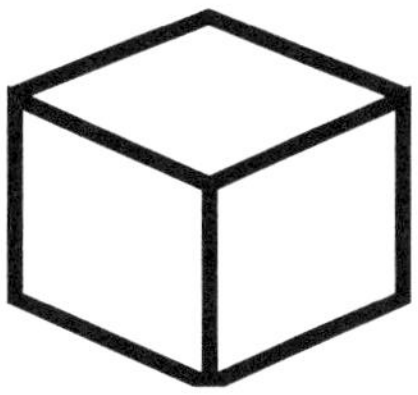

Shape of face ____________

2. Cylinder

Shape of face ____________

3. Cone

Shape of face ____________

4. Rectangular Prism

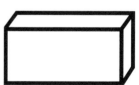

Shape of face ____________

0-7682-2912-X *Fast Ideas for Busy Teachers: Math*

Geometric Solids

Comparing Solids

Divide students into pairs and give each pair a copy of "Geometric Solids" and construction paper. Have each pair draw a line dividing the paper in half. Ask students to think of ways to separate the solids into two groups. For example, they might use the trait of having a circular face or the ability to roll.

Students should cut out the pictures of the solids and glue them onto the two halves of the construction paper. Afterwards, have students show their pictures while the rest of the class guesses which trait they used to make the groupings.

Geometric Architecture

Display pictures of cathedrals, castles, state capital buildings, sports domes, and other interesting examples of architecture. Students will be intrigued to see how cylinders, pyramids, and other solids combine to create beautiful and impressive structures.

Slide, Stack, Roll

Have students work in groups to discover which solids will slide, stack, or roll. To do this, instruct students to test each solid on a smooth, flat surface, such as a tabletop or floor. Have students record their findings on a sheet of paper. Later, discuss the results with the class to make a class chart.

Solid	Does it slide?	Does it stack?	Does it roll?
Cube	yes	yes	no
Rectangular Prism	yes	yes	no
Cone	yes	no	yes
Sphere	no	no	yes
Cylinder	yes	yes	yes
Pyramid	yes	no	no

Robot Fun

Ask parents to contribute objects such as paper towel rolls, paper cups, film canisters, cereal boxes, plastic lids, foil, and other scrap materials for building robots. Students can tape, glue, or staple pieces together to form the robot. When the robots are complete, students can write descriptions of their robots, including information on how many different geometric solids they used.

Set up the robots and their descriptions in a corner of the room for a lively display.

Name ______________________________ Date ____________

Geometric Solids

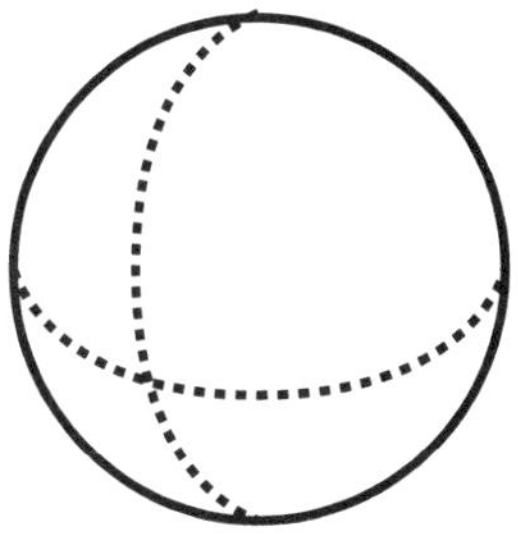

Sphere

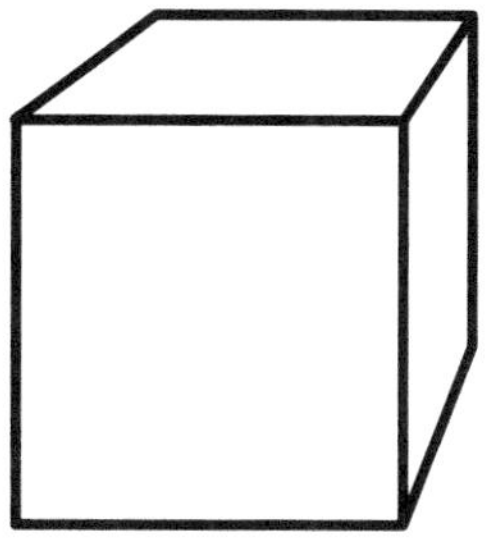

Cube

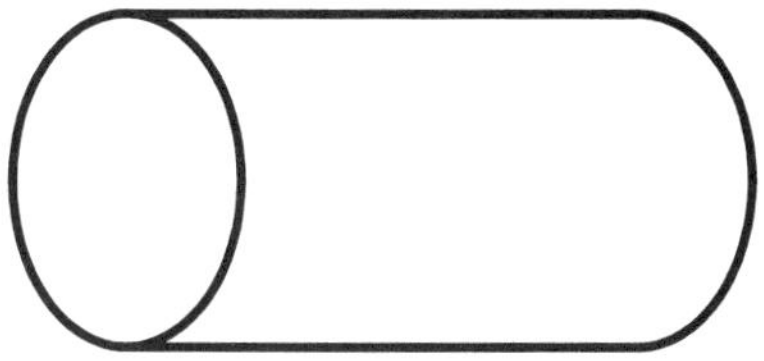

Cylinder

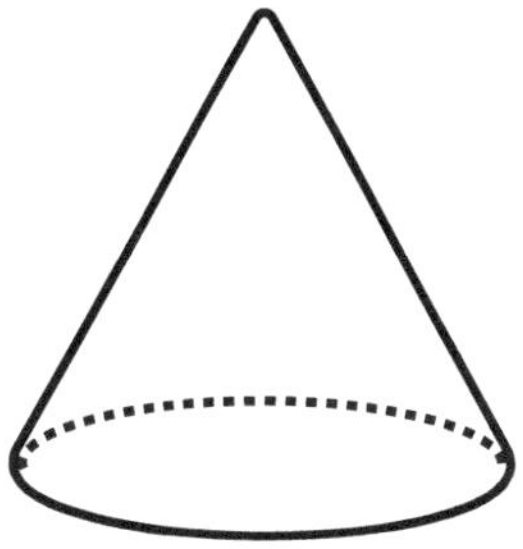

Cone

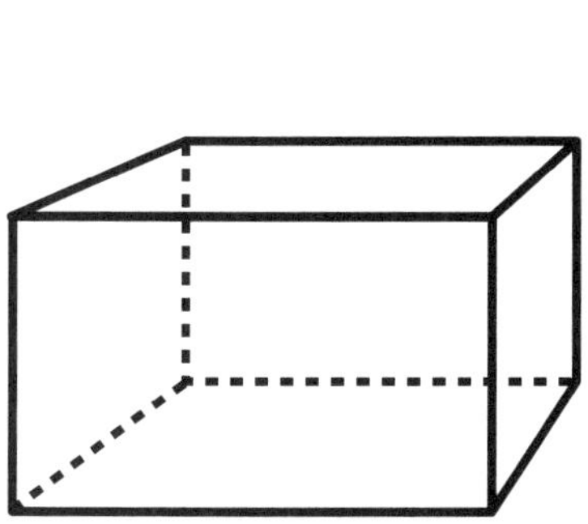

Rectangular Prism

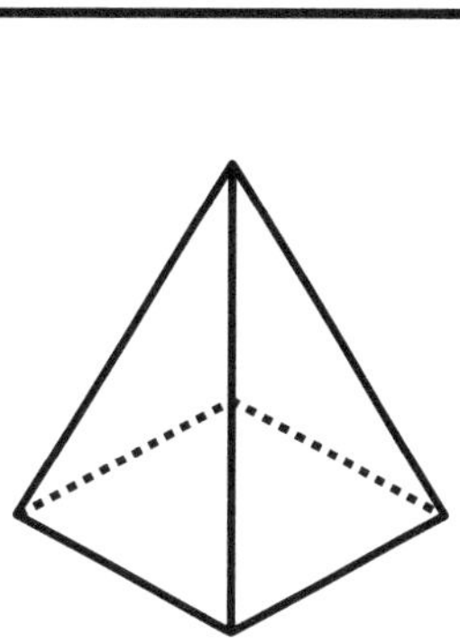

Pyramid

Fractions

Stand Up/Sit Down

This quick game reinforces the concept of equal parts. Prepare 12 or more picture cards featuring simple shapes divided into equal or unequal parts. One card might show a heart with a vertical line dividing the shape in half. Another card might show a heart with a horizontal line dividing the shape into two unequal parts. Include a variety of fractional parts, such as halves, thirds, fourths, and eighths.

Show the class one card at a time. If the card shows a shape divided into equal parts, the class stands. If the card features unequal parts, the class sits. Continue the game using all of the cards.

Fraction Match

Make a set of cards displaying fractions (such as $\frac{1}{4}$) and a set of cards displaying shapes divided into corresponding fractional parts. Number the backs of the cards so that matching cards have the same numbers. Leave the cards at a center where students can practice matching the shapes with the corresponding fractions. Students can check their work by looking at the backs of the cards.

Parts of a Group

Give each student 12 counters and six half-sheets of paper. Tell students to lay two sheets on their desks and divide the counters into two equal groups on the sheets. Ask:

How many counters are on each sheet? (6)

What fraction describes the six counters in relation to the total number? ($\frac{1}{2}$)

Why? (There are two groups of six counters each; the six counters represent one half of the total group.)

Discuss how fractions can describe parts of a group or set.

Have students lay out three sheets and divide the counters into three equal groups. Again, ask how many counters are on each sheet (4), what fraction describes each group ($\frac{1}{3}$) and why. (There are three equal groups of four counters each. The four counters on a sheet represent one-third of the total group.) Repeat the procedure with four sheets (fourths) and six sheets (sixths).

Follow-Up Activity:

Give each student a copy of "Balloon Fun." After students complete the activity, ask them to share how they solved the equations on the page.

Answers to "Balloon Fun":

red balloons–6; blue balloons–3; yellow balloons–2

Name ______________________________ Date ______________

Balloon Fun

Zippy Clown has 12 balloons.

Color $\frac{1}{2}$ of the balloons red.

Color $\frac{1}{3}$ of the balloons blue.

Color $\frac{1}{6}$ of the balloons yellow.

How many balloons are red? ______

How many balloons are blue? ______

How many balloons are yellow? ______

Fractions

Fraction Flowers

Give each student a copy of "Fraction Flowers." Students can color the flower petals any color they wish. Then instruct them to cut out each card and glue it to a half-sheet of paper. Next to the flower, tell them to write fractions that describe how they colored the flowers. For example, if a flower with five petals has two red petals and three yellow petals, a student would write:

Red $= \frac{2}{5}$

Yellow $= \frac{3}{5}$

Afterwards, have students assemble their sheets, add front and back covers, and staple them together to create "Fraction Flowers" booklets.

Food Fractions

Using food is a fun (and tasty) way for students to apply their understanding of fractions. Have the class help you cut sandwiches in halves or fourths, slice an orange into sections, or divide a loaf into equal parts. Seeing how people use fractions in everyday life makes the math experience more meaningful to students.

How Much Is a Tenth?

To develop the concept of tenths, put ten small, colored candies on a paper plate. Point out that the plate of candies has ten parts, called "tenths." Ask a student to count the number of red candies on the plate. Write the corresponding fraction on the board. For example, if there were three red candies, write $3/10$. Explain that $3/10$ means the same as "three out of ten."

Repeat the activity with the other colors of candies on the plate. For a tasty follow-up, give each student ten pieces of candy. After they write fractions to describe the different colors of candies, they can enjoy their sweet treats.

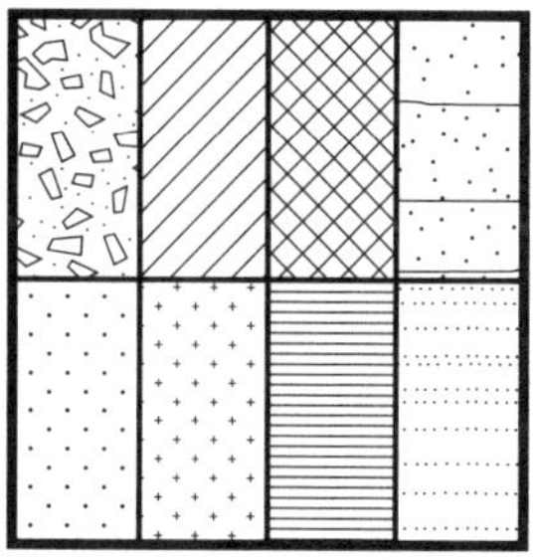

Folded Fraction Designs

Show students how to fold paper squares or circles in halves, fourths, and eighths. Have them draw lines along the fold lines so that the equal parts are distinct. Then have them use markers or crayons to color each fractional part with a different color or decorate each part with an interesting design. Arrange the designs on a bulletin board under the headings "Halves," "Fourths," or "Eighths."

Name ______________________________ Date ______________

Fraction Flowers

Telling Time

Set Your Clocks

Have each student make a clock from a small paper plate, two construction paper strips, and a brad fastener. Make a clock for yourself, as well. Then use the clocks with the following activities:

Set your clock to a time without showing the class. Say the time and have students set their clocks. Have students hold up their clocks and check if they match yours.

Write a time on the board. Have students set their clocks to match.

Write a time on the board. Have students set their clocks to show the time one hour before or after. Continue with intervals of two or more hours, a half hour, quarter hour, and five minutes.

Comparing Times

Call on five students to stand in front of the class with their paper plate clocks. Ask them to set their clocks to show what time they get up and show their clocks to the class. Ask:

Who gets up earliest?

What time does that student get up?

Who gets up latest?

What time does that student get up?

How many students get up before 7:00?

How many students get up after 7:00?

Repeat the procedure with five other students and a different activity, such as going to school or eating dinner.

Sticky Note Time

Help students tell time in five-minute intervals with this simple trick. On self-sticking notes, write 0, 5, 10, 15, 20, and so on. Place the notes in their correct positions on the outer rim of the classroom clock. To tell the time, students determine the hour and then count by fives to calculate the minutes.

Telling Time

Checking the Time

This take-home activity helps students realize how often people check the time. For one whole day on the weekend, have students and their families write down each time they look at a watch or clock and the reasons why they did so. (Examples: *8:15–I wanted to see if I had to get ready for my soccer game; 11:00–I looked to see how long until lunch.*) At the end of the day, have students tally how often their families checked the time. When students bring their papers to school, discuss the results with the class.

Analog and Digital

Familiarize students with both digital and analog clocks by providing samples of both types for the class to compare. Let students practice setting times on both clocks.

Times in My Day

Give each student a copy of "Times in My Day." Have students write the times for each activity and draw hands on the clocks to match. Afterwards, let students compare their times with classmates' times.

Extension Activity: Choose one of the activities, such as dinner, and make a chart displaying the different times students listed for it. Let the class make a bar graph using the information from the chart. Then have students look at the graph to answer questions.

What time do most students in our class eat dinner?

Do more students eat dinner at 5:30 or 6:30?

What is the earliest time that someone in our class eats dinner?

What is the latest time that someone in our class eats dinner?

How many hours is it from the earliest time to the latest time?

School Day Timeline

Let the class sequence the school day's activities by creating a visual timeline. First, list the day's activities on the board and the time that each activity begins. (Examples: Reading–9:00; Science–9:45; Recess–10:15; Math–10:30; Music–11:15)

Divide students into small groups and assign one of the activities to each group to illustrate by drawing a simple picture related to the activity (such as numbers for math). Have them make a label that includes the activity and time and draw a clock that corresponds to the time. String a clothesline across the front of the room and let the groups hang their pictures in chronological order with clothespins.

Name ______________________________ Date ______________

Times in My Day

Answer each question with a time. Draw the hands on the clocks to match.

1.
What time do you get up?

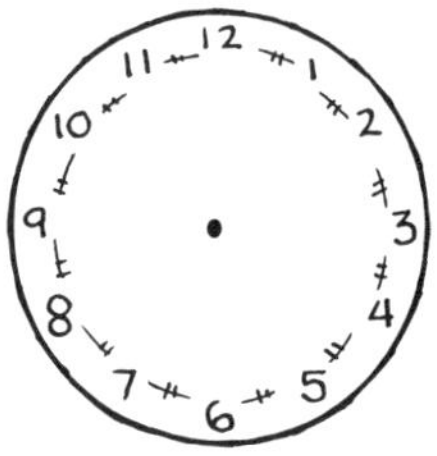

____

2.
What time do you go to school?

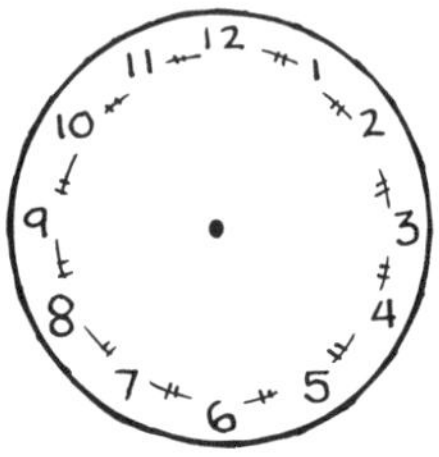

____

3.
What time do you eat lunch at school?

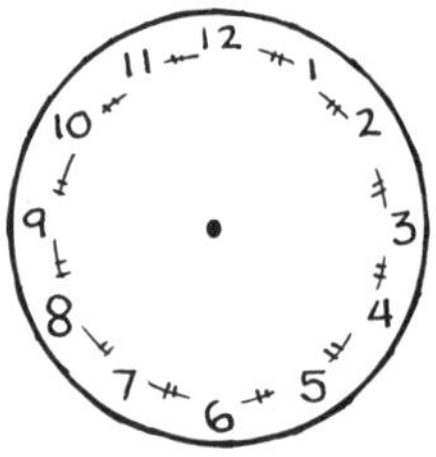

____

4.
What time do you get home from school?

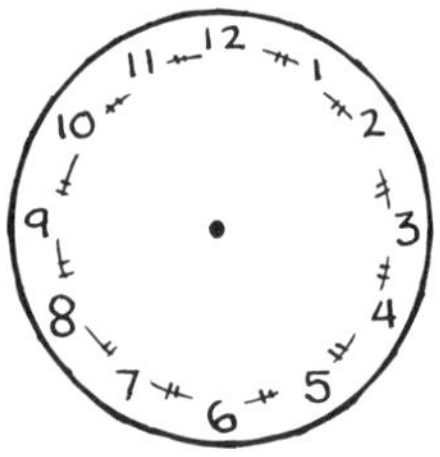

____

5.
What time do you eat dinner?

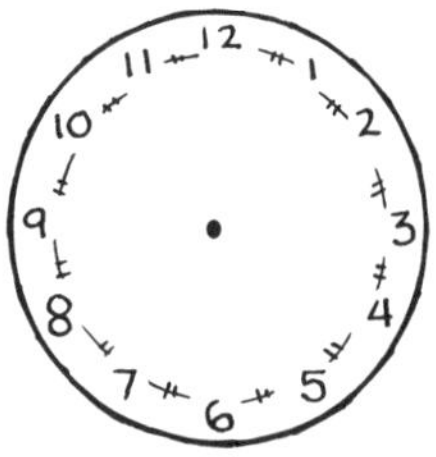

____

6.
What time do you go to bed?

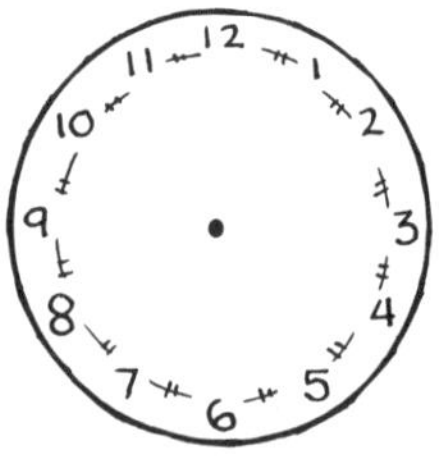

____

Look at your answers for questions 1 and 6. About how many hours is it from the time you get up to the time you go to bed? __________

Elapsed Time

Making the Most of Time

Reinforce time concepts throughout the day by having students tell the time and answer questions such as: *What time will it be in 20 minutes? What time was it ten minutes ago? How many minutes have passed since recess ended?* Students can state their answers as well as show them on their paper clocks.

A Guessing Game

This fun guessing game lets students see what they can accomplish in 5 seconds, 15 seconds, and 30 seconds.

Give each student a copy of "A Guessing Game." After students read the questions and write their guesses in the "My Guess" column, time them as they do each of the activities. Instruct students to record their results in the "My Test" column. Later, have students look over their work and circle their best guess.

TV Times

TV schedules are ideal for telling time activities. Make a copy of a schedule for each student. (It may be helpful to enlarge it on the photocopier first.) Ask questions:

What show begins on channel 4 at 6:00?

What show starts two hours later on the same channel?

How long is the movie that starts at 7:00 on channel 12?

How long would you watch TV if you saw the shows ___ and ___?

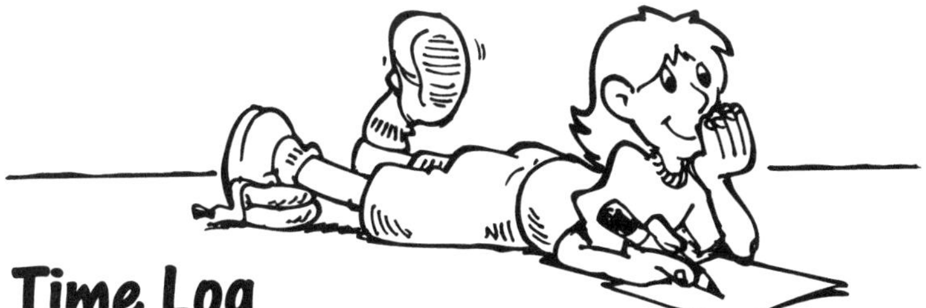

A Time Log

Talk with students about their favorite after-school activities. Have each student write the name of the activity on a sheet of paper and draw a picture of it. Ask students to keep a daily log recording how much time they spend on that activity each day for one week.

At the end of the week, have students tally their minutes (or hours) and record the amount. Then have students look through their logs and find which day they spent the most amount of time doing their activity, which day they spent the least time, and the difference between the most and the least amounts of time spent.

For an extra challenge, write the times on a chart and have students calculate the total amount of time the class as a whole spent on favorite activities.

Name ______________________ Date ____________

A Guessing Game

Read each question and write your guess in the **My Guess** column.

Have someone time you as you test your guesses.

Write the results in the **My Test** column.

In 5 seconds . . .	**My Guess**	**My Test**
How many times can you tap your feet?		
How many times can you clap your hands?		
How many times can you blink your eyes?		

In 15 seconds . . .	**My Guess**	**My Test**
How many times can you say your name?		
How high can you count by ones?		
How many letters of the alphabet can you write?		

In 30 seconds . . .	**My Guess**	**My Test**
How many times can you write your name?		
How many times can you hop on one foot?		
How many numbers can you write counting by twos?		

Calendar

Calendar Equations

Make a copy of the "My Calendar" page for each student. Have students fill in the name of the current month and dates. Ask:

What are the first and last days of the month?

What is the date of the second Friday?

What was the date three days ago?

What will the date be one week from today?

How many Saturdays are in the month?

How many Wednesdays in the month have a two in the date?

Knuckles and Dips

Show students this trick for remembering the number of days in each month. Have them make a fist with each hand and hold their hands in front of them. Tell them they will use the knuckles and "dips." Beginning with the first knuckle on the left, have students start naming the months. Each month named at a knuckle has 31 days. Each month named at a "dip" has 30 days except February. February has 28 days most years.

Date Cards

Students can practice sequencing dates with this sorting activity. Give each student five index cards. Instruct students to cut out five dates from old newspapers or magazines and mount them, one to a card. Have them arrange their cards in chronological order. After you check the order, they can write self-checking numbers on the backs. Let students trade their sets with others. Store the sets of date cards at the math center for independent practice.

Extension: Combine cards to make sets of 10, 15, 20, etc., for a more challenging activity.

Calendar Riddles

Use individual calendars or a large class calendar for this equation-solving activity. Give riddles about dates in the month and have the class look at the calendar to find the answers. Here are some examples based on January:

I'm a date in January that has a 3 in it. It's in the last week. I'm not the last day of the month. What date am I? (30)

I'm a Monday or a Wednesday. The sum of my digits is 5.
I come before January 20. What date am I? (14)

I'm a date with two digits. The sum of my digits is 10. I come after the fourth Tuesday in the month. What date am I? (28)

Name ______________________________ Date ______________

My Calendar

Write the name of the month on the line.

Fill in the numbers for the dates.

____

Month

Sunday	Monday	Tuesday	Wednesday	Thursday	Friday	Saturday

Calendar Center

Cut apart the pages of a 12-month calendar with large squares for writing and mount the individual months in order on a bulletin board to create a "Calendar Center." Ask students to mark their birthdays on the calendar. Write in holidays, important school functions such as class trips, and days off.

Write ten questions students could answer using the calendars. Examples:

Whose birthday is on ___?

How many students from our class have birthdays in January and February?

What holiday do we celebrate on the last Monday in May?

How many more days until winter break?

Students can work in small groups to answer the questions. If you wish, provide a self-checking answer key.

Missing Month Mix-Up

This game reinforces the names and sequence of the months. First, write the name of each month on a separate index card. Ask a student volunteer to step out of the classroom. Give all but one card to individual students. The 11 students who received cards stand in order at the front of the classroom holding their cards.

Tell the student who left the room to return and guess the missing month. If the student guesses correctly, she chooses the next person to leave the room. If she does not guess correctly, the correct answer is given, and she exchanges roles with the person holding the month she guessed.

Variation: Have students holding cards stand in mixed-up order at the front of the room. When the student makes the guess, the 11 students rearrange themselves in order and the student who made the guess joins them with the missing card.

How Long Until Your Birthday?

Read aloud *Birthday Rhymes, Special Times,* a collection of humorous poems selected by Bobbye S. Goldstein. The book contains a wide variety of birthday poems, including Jack Prelutsky's "My Birthday's in August" and Ogden Nash's "Between Birthdays."

Students can use the Calendar Center to calculate the number of days until their birthdays. Have the class determine who has the shortest wait and the longest wait, how many students have a birthday before the next school holiday, how many students have to wait more than six weeks, and so on.

Coin Combinations

Coin Sets

Make copies of the "Coin Set" page on construction paper or cardstock for each student. Students could color the pennies brown, then cut the coins apart. Students can store coin sets in envelopes or self-sealing bags to reuse for other counting and sorting activities.

Use the coins for these activities:

Show Me: Say an amount. Have students place the appropriate combinations on their desks.

Same Amount, Different Coins: Say an amount and have students place the correct number of coins on their desks. Then ask them to use a different combination to display the same amount.

Guess How Much: Draw a piggy bank on the board. Draw two or more circles in the bank to represent coins. Give students the combined value of the two coins. Then have students display the coins they think are inside the bank.

Start with Fewer

Some students will master counting money quickly, while others will need more time and help. Give the class practice counting fewer numbers of coins first, before moving on to greater amounts and combinations that are more difficult.

Coin Collection Webs

Use this activity to check students' understanding of coin values and to reinforce the idea that different coin combinations can represent the same value.

Divide the class into small groups. Have students use the coins they cut from the "Coin Set" page. Ask one student in each group to place a quarter in the middle of the group's workspace. Then ask the members of each group to use their coins to make different sets equivalent in value to the quarter. (One student might suggest two dimes and one nickel, while another student might suggest five nickels.)

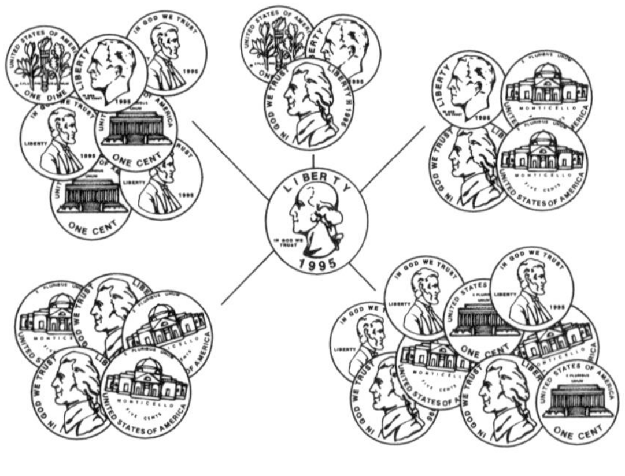

Give each group a 12" x 18" sheet of paper to use to make a web showing the coin combinations they made. Repeat the procedure with a half dollar. Later, display the different webs on a bulletin board so groups can compare their work.

Coin Set

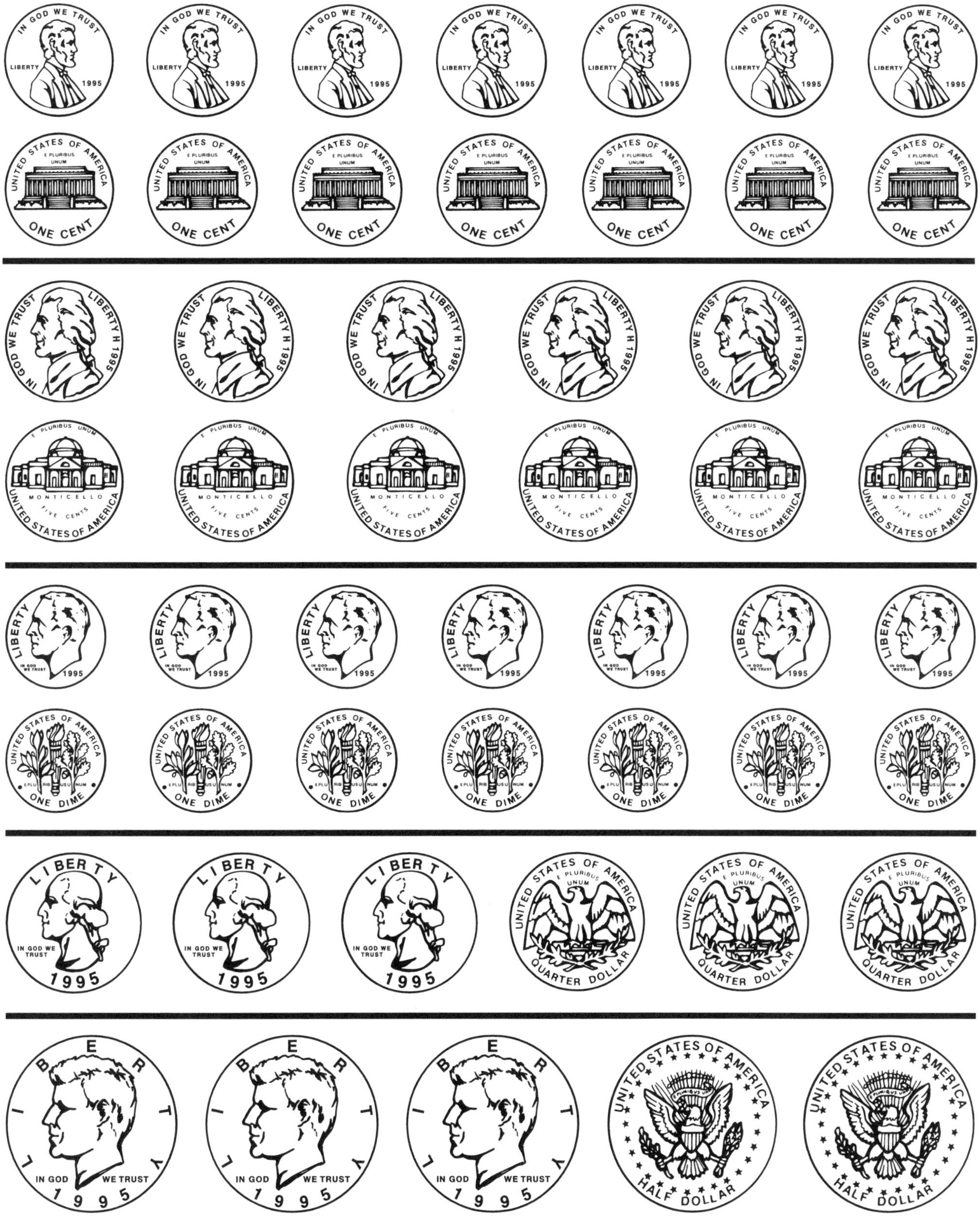
IN GOD WE TRUST
LIBERTY
1995
UNITED STATES OF AMERICA
E PLURIBUS UNUM
ONE CENT
MONTICELLO
FIVE CENTS
ONE DIME
QUARTER DOLLAR
HALF DOLLAR

Counting Coins

Money Card Game

Cut out 3" x 4" cards from cardstock. Give each student ten cards and a copy of the "Coin Set" page. Have students cut out coins and glue two to six coins onto each card to make varying amounts. Divide the class into groups of two to four players. Students in each group combine their cards. Explain how to play the game.

1. The dealer shuffles all the cards and hands them out facedown to each player. Players keep their cards facedown in a pile.
2. For each round, players turn their top cards faceup and state the value.
3. The player with the highest value collects all the cards played in the round.
4. If two players tie for the highest value, they each turn over another card. The player with the higher value wins all cards played in that round.
5. A player is out of the game if he loses all his cards. The game continues until one player wins all the cards. If time runs out, the player with the most cards wins.

Mental Calculations

As students become familiar with money, give them practice calculating amounts mentally. How much are three dimes and a nickel worth? What coins can you use to buy something that costs 75 cents? These types of equations promote mathematical thinking and help students apply real-life skills.

What's in the Bank?

Make a copy of "What's in the Bank?" on construction paper or cardstock for each student. Students should cut out three or more coins from the "Coin Set" page and glue them to the blank piggy banks.

On the lined piggy bank, each student writes clues about the coins in his bank. (Example: I have four coins. They add up to 50 cents.)

Instruct students to cut apart the piggy bank cards. Divide students into groups. Students take turns reading their clues to the group. Members of the group use the clues to guess the coins in the bank. When they finish, they check the piggy bank with the coins.

Variation:

Give each student an envelope. Ask them to put the card with the piggy bank and coins inside the envelope and glue or tape the card with the clues to the front of the envelope. Store the cards in a small box in the math center with play coins. Encourage students to manipulate play coins to figure out the clues, then open the envelopes and check their answers. If you prefer, read several of the clues aloud each day and have the class work together to figure out what coins are in the banks.

What's in the Bank?

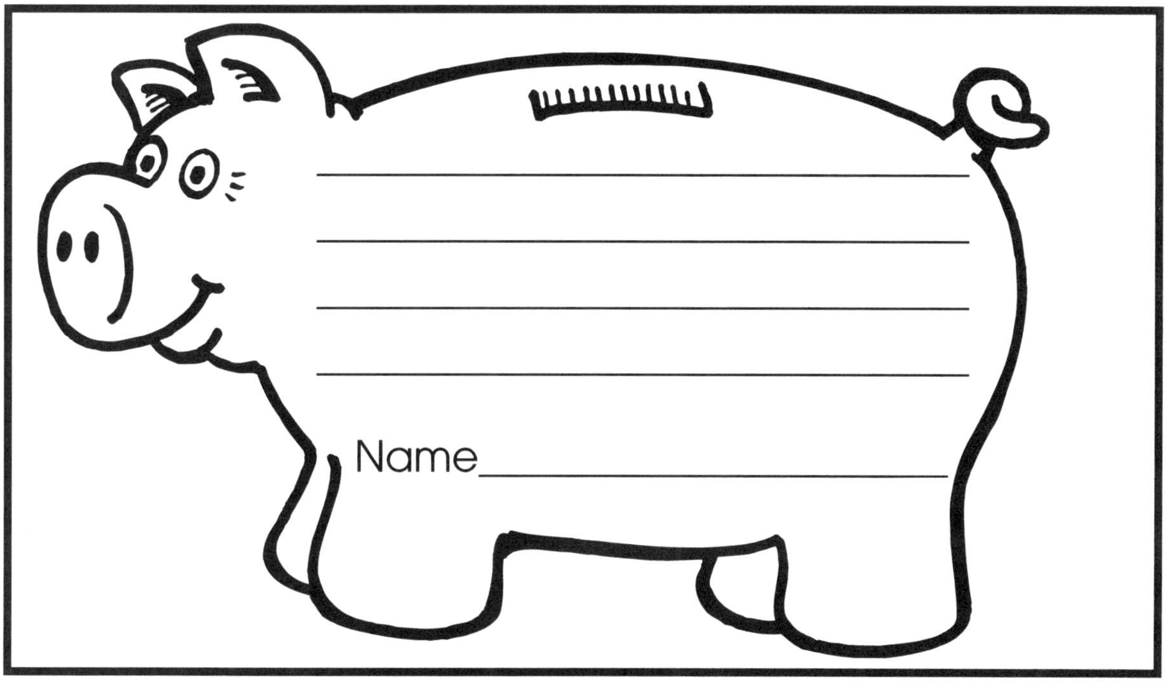

Place Value and Adding and Subtracting Money

Place Value Mats

Give each student a 12" x 18" sheet of yellow paper. Have students glue a 9" x 12" sheet of orange paper on the left-hand side of the paper. Instruct students to label the yellow half *Ones* and the orange half *Tens.*

Students can use their mats and a set of dimes and pennies or paper coins cut from the "Coin Set" page with the addition and subtraction activities on this page.

Adding and Subtracting Cents

Write 23¢ + 14¢ vertically on the board. Tell students to place the corresponding coins on their mats: two dimes in the tens column and three pennies in the ones column, then place a dime and four pennies in the appropriate columns. Instruct the class to add up the coins. Call on a student to write the answer on the board. Remind the class to include the cent sign. Continue the activity with other addition equations.

Five-Equation Warm-Up

Each day, write five addition or subtraction equations involving money on the board. Use the equations as a warm-up activity first thing in the morning or at the start of math class. Then have students check their work together. To make the activity more motivating, divide the class into teams. Students who answer all five equations correctly earn one point for the team.

At the end of a given period, total the points for each team. The team with the most points earns a small prize, such as a one-day homework pass for math, lunch with the teacher, or other appropriate treat.

Variation:

Repeat the activity with subtraction equations. Begin by writing a subtraction equation vertically on the board, such as 49¢ – 15¢. Have students place the corresponding number of coins on their mats and then have them take away the appropriate coins.

Place Value and Adding and Subtracting Money

Note: Students will need place value mats (see description on previous page) and pennies and dimes or paper coins cut from the "Coin Set" page for the first two activities below.

Regroup and Add

Write 17¢ + 26¢ vertically on the board. Have students place the corresponding coins on their place value mats. Then guide the class through the following steps to find the answer:

1. Add the pennies (13).
2. Take ten of the pennies and trade them for a dime.
3. Move the dime to the tens section. (There will be three pennies left in the ones column.)
4. Add the dimes (4).

Ask a student to write the answer on the board (43¢). Repeat the activity with other addition equations involving regrouping.

From Right to Left

Show students that adding and subtracting cents is similar to adding and subtracting two-digit numbers. Write money equations vertically using the cent symbol and ask the class what similarities they see. Remind students to add or subtract the numbers in the right column first before moving on to the numbers on the left.

Regroup and Subtract

Tell students: Kyle had 53 cents. He spent 28 cents. How much money did he have left?

Ask a student to write the corresponding equation vertically on the board. Then have students use their place value mats and coins to illustrate the equation.

Begin by having them place five dimes and three pennies on their mats. Remind students that they need to subtract from the ones column first. Students will see that they cannot subtract eight pennies from three. Guide them into taking a dime from the tens column and replacing it with ten pennies. Have them place the ten pennies in the ones column.

Now they can subtract the eight pennies and then the two dimes. Ask how many dimes and pennies remain (two dimes and five pennies) and have a student write the answer on the board.

Repeat the activity with other subtraction math stories involving regrouping.

Adding and Subtracting Money

Worksheet Pattern

Use the "Let's Go to the Bank" page to create custom-made review activities of addition and subtraction concepts with your class. Fill in the blank path with equations appropriate to the level of your class and the skill being taught in the current unit. Then make a copy for each student.

Here are some ideas:

Write vertical addition equations with or without regrouping.

Write vertical subtraction equations with or without regrouping.

Write a mixture of addition and subtraction equations.

Let students write their own equations on the sheet and include an answer key. Then have students exchange papers with a partner and solve each other's equations.

Students Write the Questions

Students enjoy creating equations and math stories for classmates to solve. Students can write their suggestions on slips of paper and place them in a box. Sort through the suggestions and use them for warm-ups or group activities.

Occasionally create a review test composed entirely of student-suggested material.

Let's Go to the Bank Game

Use the "Let's Go to the Bank" page as a game board. Pair up students and give each pair a copy of the page. Ask each student to write money equations on ten index cards and provide an answer key.

Students should mix their equation cards together and place them facedown. Players take turns taking the top card, solving for the answer on a sheet of paper, and moving a marker on the path if the answer is correct. The student who reaches the bank by solving exactly 12 equations wins. (Both players can win in this situation.)

Name ______________________ Date ____________

Let's Go to the Bank

Help the children get to the bank.

Write the answers to the equations on the path.

0-7682-2912-X *Fast Ideas for Busy Teachers: Math*

Place Value to 1,000

Let's Match

Work with a small group around a table. Divide a large sheet of paper into three columns labeled *Hundreds, Tens,* and *Ones.* Arrange place value blocks or other manipulatives representing hundreds, tens, and ones in the columns. Have students state the number of hundreds, tens, and ones. Ask a volunteer to write the matching number on the board. (If there were 3 hundreds, 7 tens, and 5 ones, the student would write 375.)

Ask the student to state the value of each number and explain what it represents. (The 5 represents the number of ones, the 7 represents the number of tens, and the 3 represents the number of hundreds.) Repeat the activity several times with other numbers.

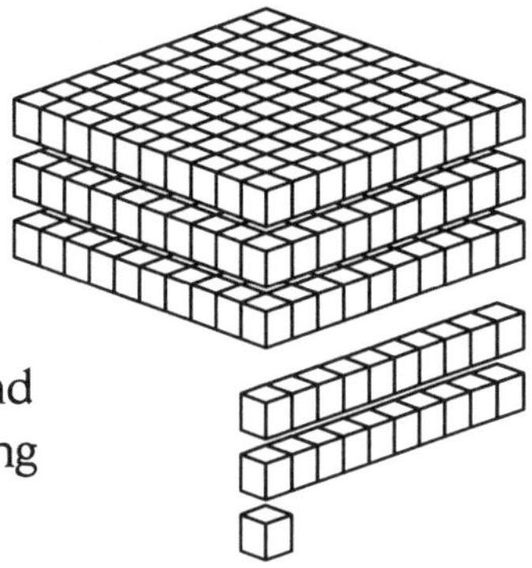

Variation:

Change the activity by writing a three-digit number on the board and having students arrange the matching number of blocks on the paper.

Guess My Number

When the class has a few spare minutes before lunch or dismissal, play "Guess My Number." Write a three-digit number on a piece of paper. Then let students guess the number. After each guess, respond with either "greater than" or "less than" to help students formulate their next guess. Continue this procedure until a student correctly guesses the number. That student thinks of a number for the next game.

Date Digits

Challenge students to list as many two- and three-digit numbers as they can make from the digits in the current year. At the end of a time limit, have students take turns naming a number. Write each different number on the board.

As a follow-up, give each student a copy of "Date Digits" to complete at home. Students write the birth date of a family member and find two- and three-digit numbers using the digits in that date. Have students bring their papers back to school and compare their results.

Extension Activity:

Ask students to explain their strategies for finding all the possible numbers. For example, some students might write all the two-digit numbers first and the three-digit number combinations last. Others might start with one digit and make all the possible combinations beginning with that number; then start with the next digit and make all the combinations they could beginning with that number, and so on.

Name ______________________________ Date ______________

Date Digits

Write the name of a family member.

____

Write the year that person was born.

____

Use the digits in the date to make two-digit and three-digit numbers.

Write the name of another family member:

____

Write the year that person was born:

____

Use the digits in the date to make two-digit and three-digit numbers.

Place Value to 1,000 and Comparing and Ordering Numbers to 1,000

Place the Digits

This fun game develops skills in place value and comparison of three-digit numbers. You will need a set of number cards from 0 to 9 and a small paper bag. Have students divide a sheet of lined paper into three columns and label the columns from left to right: *Hundreds, Tens,* and *Ones.*

Select a number card from the bag and call out the number. Each student writes that number in any of the three columns. Do not return the card to the bag. Repeat the procedure with two more numbers.

Ask a student to say the three-digit number he made and write it on the board. Call on other students until all the different numbers they made are written on the board. (There are six possibilities for each set of three numbers.)

The students who made the highest number win one point and make a tally mark at the bottom of the page. Return the number cards to the bag and play another round. Continue until one student earns a total of ten points.

Visualizing Large Numbers

Students may have a difficult time visualizing large numbers. To help them, give the class opportunities to make collections of pictures or objects representing numbers greater than 100. For example, students can use rubber stamps to stamp out groups of 100 or glue beans or macaroni to cardboard squares to make sets of 100.

Three-Digit Puzzlers

Call out three digits. Students should write the three digits on a piece of paper and rearrange the numbers to create six 3-digit numbers. Have students circle the largest number and cross out the smallest number.

Variations:

Ask students to rewrite the three-digit numbers in order from least to greatest or greatest to least.

Make the activity more challenging by specifying whether the three-digit numbers they write must be odd or even.

Comparing and Ordering Numbers to 1,000

Note: Write a different three-digit number on 20 to 30 index cards to use with the next three activities.

Beat My Number

Place the three-digit number cards in a bag and divide the class into two teams. One player from each team takes a card from the bag and reads the number. The player with the greater number keeps both cards. Continue playing until every student has taken a card from the bag. The team with the most cards wins.

Use Manipulatives

If students are uncertain about which of two 3-digit numbers is greater (for example, if they could not distinguish between 245 and 254), have them use place value blocks to represent both numbers, then compare the two.

Number Line-Up

Give one 3-digit number card to each student. Call on five students at a time to stand in front of the class and arrange themselves so that their cards appear in order from the least to the greatest. Repeat the procedure until all students have had a chance to line up in front of the class.

Number Line-Up Relay

Divide the class into two teams and line up each team behind a table. Place five number cards facedown in a pile on each table. At your signal, the first five players each take a number card and arrange themselves in order from the least number to the greatest. The five players who line up in order first score a point for their team. Mix up all the cards between the groups and repeat with the next five students on each team. Continue until one team scores five points to win.

Sky-High Numbers

Give each student a copy of "Sky-High Numbers." Instruct students to write three digits on each set of clouds. At least two of the three digits must be different. After students complete the activity, discuss the following questions with the class:

If you used three different digits, how many numbers could you make? (6)

If you used only two different digits, how many numbers could you make? (3)

Why can you make fewer numbers when you use only two different digits? (The number combinations are limited because you'd repeat combinations when two of the three digits are the same.)

Name ______________________________ Date ______________

Sky-High Numbers

Write a digit on each cloud. For each set of clouds, write as many three-digit numbers as you can using the numbers on the clouds. Then circle the greatest number and underline the least number on each banner.

A.

B.

C.

0-7682-2912-X *Fast Ideas for Busy Teachers: Math*

Place Value and Adding and Subtracting Three-Digit Numbers

Addition and Subtraction Relays

Divide the class into teams. Have a member of each team go to the board. State an addition or subtraction equation for the team members to solve. Other students work the equations on paper. The first person at the board to solve the equation correctly scores a point for his team. If no one at the board has the correct answer, have them all try again. Repeat the activity several times. The team with the most points wins.

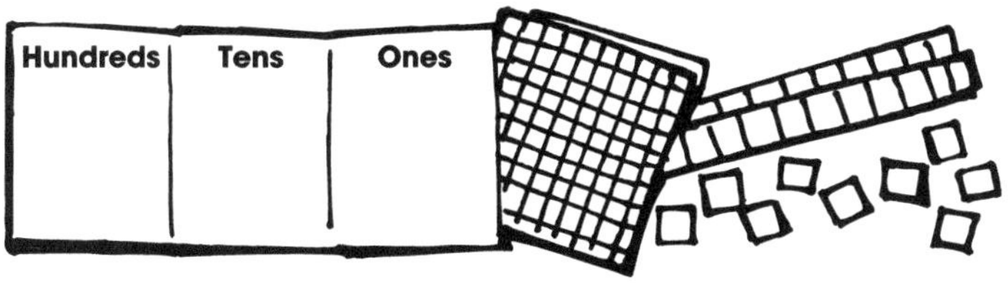

Line Up the Digits

When writing equations involving three-digit numbers, students may have trouble lining up the numbers to add or subtract. To help them line up the columns correctly, let them write their equations on one-inch grid paper.

Working with Place Value Mats

Give each student a 12" x 18" sheet of light-colored construction paper that has been folded into thirds. Instruct students to trace on the fold lines to make three columns and label them *Hundreds, Tens,* and *Ones.*

Give each student three copies of the "Hundred-Blocks and Ten-Strips" page. Have students cut out the manipulatives. They can use small paper squares for ones. Use the materials for the following activities:

How Many in All? Tell the class to set out five hundreds, three tens, and two ones on their mats. Then have them add three more tens and seven ones. Ask how many squares there are in all (569). Ask a student to write an addition equation on the board to represent what they did. (532 + 37 = 569) Repeat the activity with other equations. Later, have students solve three-digit subtraction equations in the same way.

Solve the Math Story: Give the class a math story, such as *There were 325 students in the cafeteria. Then 142 more students walked in. How many students were in the cafeteria altogether?* Have the class set out the appropriate number of squares and solve the equation.

Regrouping Skills: Use the materials to teach regrouping skills. For example, when adding 138 + 245, students first combine the 8 ones and 5 ones to get 13 ones. Then they trade ten ones for a ten-strip and move the strip to the tens columns. Then they add the tens and hundreds to find the sum. When subtracting numbers like 542 – 36, students trade a ten-strip for ten ones and move them to the ones column before subtracting.

Hundred-Blocks and Ten-Strips

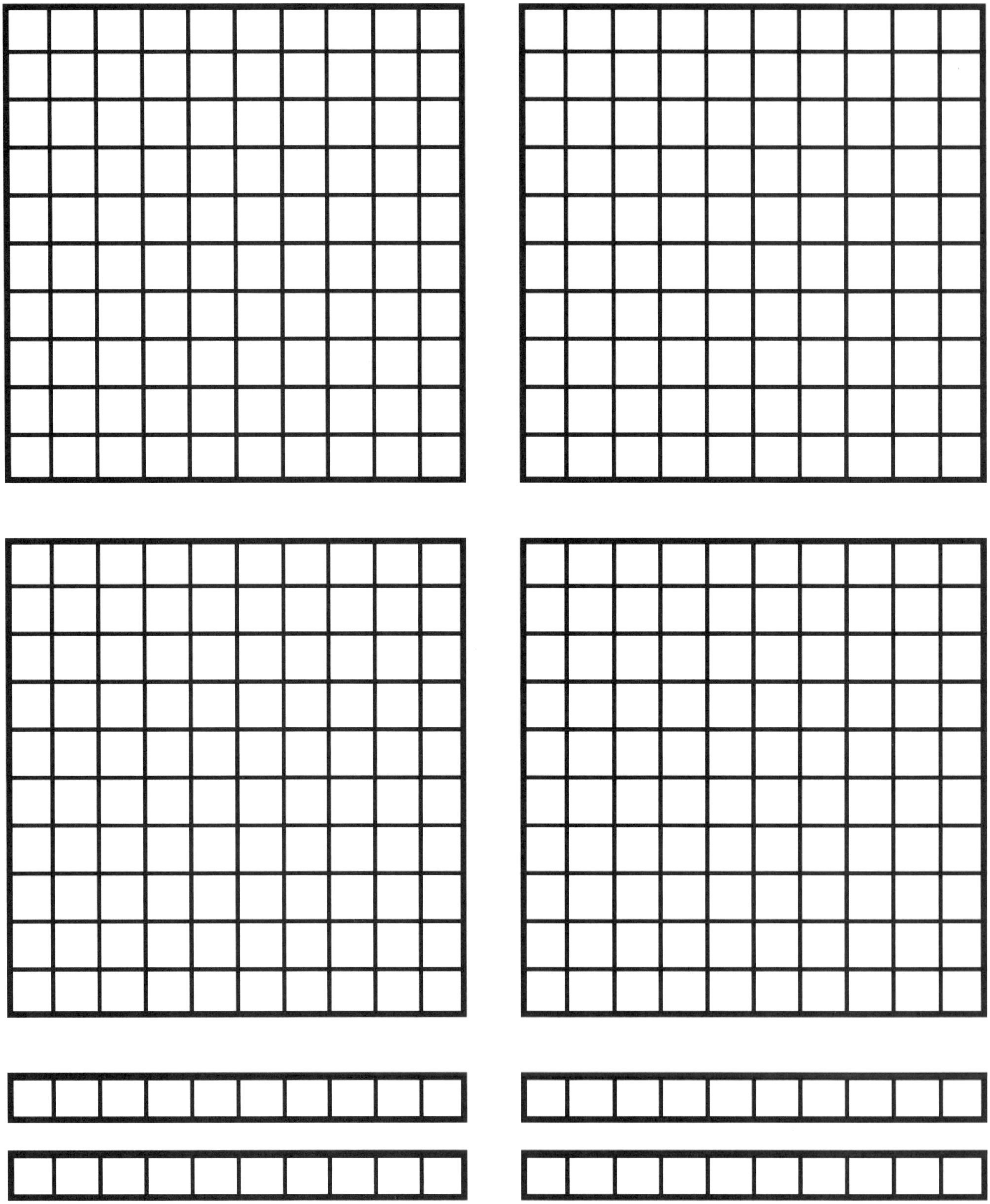

Adding and Subtracting Three-Digit Numbers

Shoe Box Pitch

This game helps develop math concepts, as well as coordination skills. To prepare, tape three shoe boxes together and label them *Hundreds, Tens,* and *Ones*. Students will also need paper, pencils, and eight to ten small beanbags.

Let four or five students at a time play "Shoe Box Pitch." Place two strips of masking tape on the floor several feet apart to show where to place the shoe boxes and where students should stand. Players take turns throwing two beanbags into the boxes.

When all players finish, the group counts the beanbags in each box to determine the first number for the math part of the game. If there were three beanbags in the hundreds box, six in the tens box, and one in the ones box, the first number would be 361.

Each player writes that number on a sheet of paper. Players repeat the procedure to get the second number and write it below the first number. The group decides whether to add or subtract the numbers. Players solve the equation and check one another's answers before moving on to the next equation.

Personal Math Stories

Give each student an index card. Ask students to write a math story involving three-digit numbers that uses themselves as the character in the story. Give them an example: ______ read 321 pages in March and 245 pages in April. How many pages did she read in all?

They should write the answers on the backs of the cards. Collect the cards and store them in a file box. Each day read two or three math stories to the class. Students can solve them for a quick review.

Moving Along

Make two or three sets of the "Car Patterns" on colored paper. Cut out the cards and laminate them. With a permanent marker, write an addition or subtraction equation in the center of each car. Display the car cards in a row on a table or bulletin board. (To remove the equations and reuse the cards, use nail polish remover and a damp paper towel.)

Give each student a copy of the "Car Patterns" page. Have students choose six of the equations and copy them on their cars. When they finish, check their answers. Have them correct any errors. They can color the cars and cut them out. Have each student draw a wide, curved road on a 6" x 24" sheet of white butcher paper, then glue their cars onto the road. Display the "roads" on your bulletin board under the title, "Moving Along in Math."

Car Patterns

Counting Coins and Bills

What Makes a Dollar?

Give students play coins or sets of paper coins cut from the "Coin Set" page. Hold up a dollar bill. Remind students that a dollar is worth 100 cents. Ask: *How many pennies equal a dollar?*

Have students lay out one dime at a time and count by tens to 100. Ask: *How many dimes equal a dollar?* Repeat the activity with nickels, quarters, and half dollars.

As a follow-up, give each student a copy of "What Makes a Dollar?" Instruct students to draw four other coin combinations that equal one dollar. Divide students into groups. Have them use the answers on their sheet to make a group chart showing different coin combinations equal to one dollar.

Bags of Money

Keep self-sealing plastic bags with different amounts of coins and bills in the math center. Have pairs of students choose a different bag each day to count and write the amount of money in the bag. Provide an answer key so students can check their work.

Dollar Race

This game reinforces counting coins to one dollar. Pair up students and give each pair a paper bag containing ten pennies, four nickels, five dimes, two quarters, and one half dollar. Include more coins if you prefer.

Players take turns shaking the bag and selecting a coin without looking. They draw the coin on paper and return it to the bag. Players continue until one player's total equals one dollar or more.

Dollar Sets

Make a copy of the "Dollar Bills" page on green construction paper for each student. Students cut out the dollar bills and use them with paper or play coins for these activities:

Match the Amount: Say an amount, such as $1.45. Have students set out the appropriate amount of money on their desks.

Money Math Stories: State an addition or subtraction story involving money. (Leslie has $1.30. She earned 30 more cents. How much money does Leslie have now?) Have students use their money to show the answer.

Equivalent Amounts: Ask one student to set out a dollar bill and one or more coins on his desk and state the total amount. Other members of the class make the same amount using a different combination of bills and coins.

Name ______________________________ Date ______________

What Makes a Dollar?

Draw four different sets of coins that equal one dollar.

A.	B.
C.	D.

Dollar Bills

Writing Dollars and Cents

How Much Money?

Students will need sets of play or paper coins and bills for this activity. Tell them to set out a dollar bill and a quarter on their desks. Ask: How much money is there in all? Write the amount on the board. ($1.25)

Ask: What do you notice about the way I've written the amount? (There's a period between the 1 and 25. There's a dollar sign to the left of the 1.) If the term is new, introduce them to the term *decimal point*. Have students set out another dollar bill and a dime. Ask a volunteer to write the new amount on the board. ($2.35)

Continue the activity with other students and different amounts of money. For amounts involving bills and one nickel, point out that they should write 05 after the decimal point. Explain that the zero is a placeholder to show you have 5 cents instead of 50 cents.

As a follow-up, students can work in pairs, taking turns showing bills and coins while their partners write the amounts on paper.

Which Is More?

Write $1.35 and $1.53 on the board. Have students show each amount using their sets of coins and bills. Point out that the 3 and 5 in $1.35 mean something different from the 3 and 5 in $1.53. Review what each of the numbers in the decimal notation means. (In $1.35, the 1 refers to the number of dollars, the 3 refers to the number of dimes, and the 5 refers to the number of pennies.) Ask a student to go to the board and circle the greater amount. Repeat the procedure with other amounts of money.

Money Mats

Have each student make a money mat by gluing a 9" x 12" sheet of orange paper to the left side of a 12" x 18" sheet of yellow paper.

Next, have them draw a line down the middle of the yellow side and label the far right column *Pennies*, the middle column *Dimes*, and the left (orange) column *Dollars*. Students can use their money mats with sets of coins and bills for the activities on the next page.

Dollars	Dimes	Pennies

Adding Dollars and Cents

Note: Students can use their "Money Mats" (see previous page) with sets of coins and bills for these activities.

Adding and Subtracting Money: Write $2.35 + $1.10 vertically on the board. Point out how the decimal points line up. Ask students to place two dollars, three dimes, and five pennies on their mats in the correct columns. Then add one more dollar and one more dime in the appropriate columns. Students count to find the total amount. ($3.45) Ask a student to write the answer on the board. Continue with other equations.

Review the addition process with students, reminding them to add pennies first, dimes next, and dollars last. Help them see that adding dollars and cents is like adding three-digit numbers. Use a similar procedure for teaching how to subtract money.

Money Sums: Pair up students and give each pair a copy of "Money Sums." Have students cut out the number cards at the bottom of the page and take turns using them to make addition equations. Encourage them to use their money mats and sets of coins and bills to solve the equations.

Regrouping Money: Write $5.27 + $2.06 on the board. Have students place their dollars, dimes, and pennies on their mats to show $5.27 and then place two more dollars and six pennies on the mats. When they add the pennies, they will probably notice there are 13 pennies in the pennies column.

Ask: *What should we do with the 13 pennies?* (Trade ten pennies for one dime and move the dime to the dimes column.) Then students can add the dimes and dollars to finish solving the equation. Continue with other addition equations.

Write $3.56 – $1.37 vertically on the board. Have students show $3.56 on their mats. Ask them how they can subtract $1.37 when there are only six pennies in the ones column. (They first need to trade a dime for ten pennies and move the coins to the pennies column.) After subtracting the pennies, they can subtract the dimes and dollars. Continue with other subtraction equations.

Find the Decimal Points

Give students copies of grocery store or other store ads. Have students highlight or circle the decimal points in the ads, then ask them to point out the number of dollars and cents to reinforce the fact that a decimal point separates the dollars from the cents.

Let students use ads to write math stories involving dollars and cents. (If I buy the notebook for $1.19 and the markers for $1.49, how much would the two items cost?)

0-7682-2912-X *Fast Ideas for Busy Teachers: Math*

Money Sums

Cut out the number cards at the bottom of the page. Make an addition equation by placing cards on the blank boxes. Write the equation on another sheet of paper. Use coins and bills to find the answers. Make at least five equations and solve them.

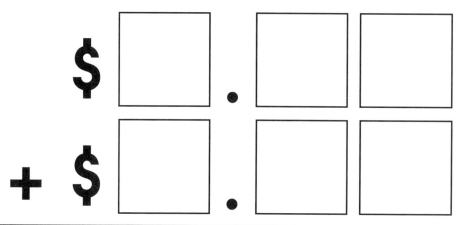

$ ☐ . ☐ ☐

\+ $ ☐ . ☐ ☐

0	1	2	3	4
5	6	7	8	9

Making Purchases

Shopping Spree

On the same day each week, post a full-page newspaper grocery ad in your classroom. Have students select three items from the ad and find the total cost. Change the ad weekly.

How Far Can Your Money Go?

Challenge students to see how far they can stretch their money. Divide the class into small groups and give each group a copy of the same grocery store flier. Without spending more than five dollars, ask groups to make grocery lists based on the flier. They should list the items, cost of each item, plus the total amount.

When they finish, let students share their lists and explain how they selected their items. Then have the class decide which group got the greatest value for their money.

As a follow-up, read Judith Viorst's *Alexander, Who Used to Be Rich Last Sunday* to the class. Students will enjoy seeing how Alexander used up all of his money in just a few days.

Real-Life Connections

Collect catalogs, store fliers, restaurant menus, and other materials that display prices to use with activities that help develop students' ability to compare prices, select items for purchase, add up prices to find the total cost, and help make connections between what they learn in class and real life.

At the Bookstore

Let students set up a bookstore in the classroom using books from your learning center or library. Preprice the books by attaching circular stickers or small pieces of masking tape to each book. Write prices between $1 and $5 on each book.

Choose a student to be the cashier. Give students a variety of play money totaling $5. Let one group at a time visit the bookstore. Each student selects a book and "pays" for it with the appropriate amount of bills and coins.

After the students from one group have visited the bookstore, they return the books for the next group to "buy." Change the cashier for each group.

While students are visiting the bookstore, the rest of the class can complete the activity "At the Card Shop."

Name ______________________________ Date ______________

At the Card Shop

Draw the bills and coins you need to buy each card.

A.  **$1.00** **25¢** $1.25	B.  $1.40
C.  $2.00	D.  $2.20
E.  $3.07	F.  $2.80
G.  $3.50	H.  $2.61

Estimating and Measuring Length

Can You Estimate?

This activity reinforces students' understanding of standard units of measurement.

Give students specific measurements (one inch, four inches, etc.), and tell them to draw lines of those specific lengths without using a ruler. When they finish, students can use a ruler to see how close they came to the actual measurements. Have them write the actual length next to each line.

Extension: Give students specific measurements in feet. Ask them to estimate that distance in the classroom, hall, gym, or playground. They can use yardsticks or tape measures to check their estimates.

Measurement Poster

Let students collect objects measuring exactly one inch, two inches, three inches, etc. Tape the objects to poster board and label their lengths so that students can see and "get a feel" for the different lengths.

Measure and Discover

Ask the class to brainstorm for ideas of items they could measure for length, width, or height. Students can suggest any object inside or outside the classroom. List their suggestions on the board.

Pair up students and have each student choose one item from the list. Provide appropriate measuring tools (rulers, yardsticks, tape measures) for students to measure and record the length of each item.

Compile the measurements on a class chart titled "Did You Know?" On it, have students list the items and sizes, beginning each statement with the phrase "Did you know . . ."

Examples: Did you know that a swing is 24 inches wide? Did you know that Josh's foot is six inches long?

Students will discover a lot about the comparative sizes of objects by looking at the chart.

Classmate Line-Up

Ask students to guess how long a line they could make if they all held hands and stretched across the playground. Write their guesses on the board. Go to the playground, gym, or a long hallway and find the answer with a tape measure while students hold hands to make their line. When they return to the classroom, students can compare their estimates to the actual measurement.

Estimating and Measuring Length

Comparing Heights and Foot-Lengths

Ask the class if they think taller students have longer feet and have them give reasons for their opinions. Pair up students. Have partners measure each other's heights in inches and record them on a chart. Students can use the chart to make a vertical bar graph showing each student's height from the shortest to the tallest. Each bar should clearly display the student's name and height.

Next, have each student trace his left foot on paper (without a shoe) and cut out the shape. Show students how to measure the length of the foot shape from the big toe to the back of the heel. They should write the length and their names on their foot shapes. Help students arrange the foot shapes from shortest to longest and glue them on a long strip of butcher paper. The heel of each foot should touch the bottom of the paper.

Discuss both displays with the class. Students will see by the order of the names that, although there are some exceptions, in general, taller students have longer feet.

Yarn Fun

Looks can be deceiving, as students will discover with this estimating activity.

Measure a four-foot length of thick yarn, a five-foot length of medium yarn, and a six-foot length of thin yarn, each a different color. Roll each length of yarn into a ball. Let students examine the three balls of yarn without unraveling them. Ask students to write the color of each ball of yarn and their estimates for the length of each one.

Unroll each ball of yarn, measure it, and record the length on the board. Ask these questions:

Which ball of yarn was the longest?

Which one was the shortest?

Which ball of yarn did you think would be the longest and why?

Why do you think the largest ball of yarn was actually the shortest when it was unrolled?

Measuring Inch by Inch

Read Leo Lionni's *Inch by Inch* to the class. Discuss how the inchworm measured the various animals in the story by traveling along their bodies. Then give each student a copy of "Measure Inch by Inch." They should use rulers to measure how far each inchworm has traveled.

Answers to "Measure Inch by Inch":
A. 3 inches B. 5 inches C. 2 inches
D. 1 inch E. 4 inches F. 6 inches G. 7 inches

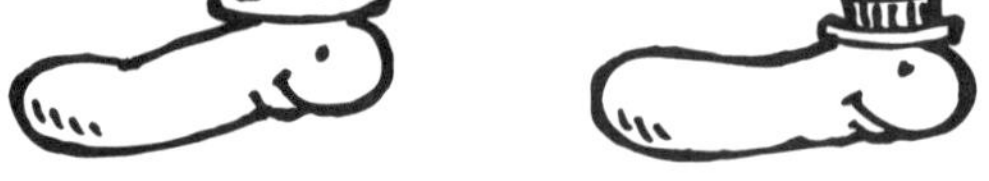

Name ______________________________ Date ______________

Measure Inch by Inch

Use a ruler marked in inches. Measure how far each inchworm has traveled.

A. ______ inches

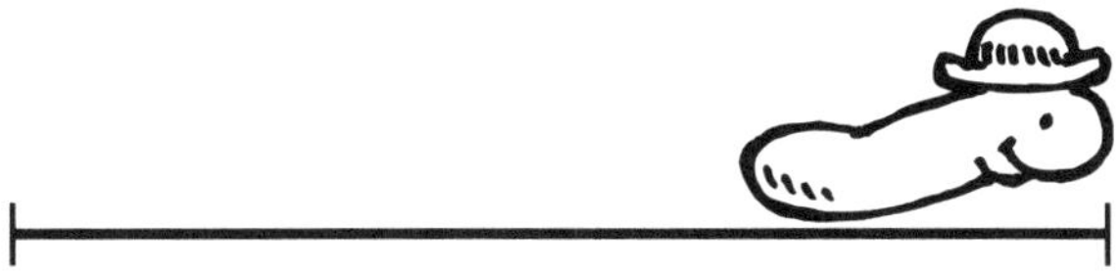

B. ______ inches

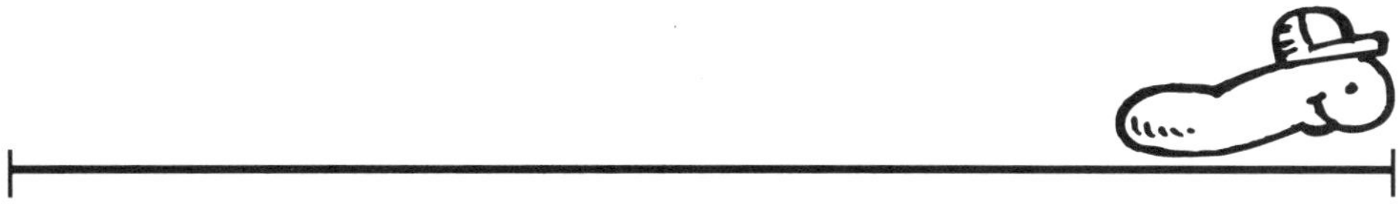

C. ______ inches

D. ______ inches

E. ______ inches

F. ______ inches

G. ______ inches

0-7682-2912-X *Fast Ideas for Busy Teachers: Math*

Estimating and Measuring Volume

Comparing Standard Units

Label four empty appropriate-sized containers: *cup, pint, quart,* and *gallon.* You could use a measuring cup, a one-pint pickle jar, a one-quart juice container, and a gallon milk jug. Tell students we use cups, pints, quarts, and gallons to measure liquids. Let students use water and the containers to find the number of cups in a pint, the number of pints in a quart, and so on. Let students record different ways of describing a measure of liquid. (Example: 1 gallon = 4 quarts = 8 pints = 16 cups; 4 pints = 8 cups; or 3 quarts = 6 pints)

Capacity

Share the book *Capacity* (Math Counts series) by Henry Pluckrose with the class. Keep a copy of the book for student reference in the math center while studying volume and capacity.

Capacity Relay Race

On a nice day, let students run a relay race on the playground to see which team can fill a pail of water first. Divide the group into teams. Provide a plastic drinking cup, small pail (one-gallon ice cream pails work great), and a tub of water for each team. Set empty pails 20 to 30 yards from the tubs of water. Have teams line up behind the tubs.

Give the first student in each line a plastic cup. On your mark, the first student from each team fills the cup with water from the tub, runs to the pail, dumps in the water, and runs back. He hands the empty cup to the next runner and goes to the end of the line.

Students continue until one team fills the pail to the brim. When they finish, ask students to discuss the strategy they used to fill the pails. Some may have filled the cup less full or run slower so they spilled less. Which strategy seemed to work best?

Estimate, Measure, and Graph

Ask students to measure the capacity of various containers, such as a bowl; a pot; a pail; a large, odd-shaped vase; and a plastic tub. Before they measure, have students agree on a unit of measure, such as pint or quart. They can draw a picture of each container and estimate how many of that unit it will hold. When they measure the actual capacity, they record their findings next to their estimates and compare their estimates to the actual capacity.

Students can make bar graphs comparing the different capacities of the containers.

Estimating and Measuring Volume

A Cup of Water

Tell students that liquids have a special property—they take the shape of their containers. This activity helps students discover that, because of this property, equal amounts of liquid look different in different-shaped containers.

Collect four clear containers: a measuring cup, large plastic drinking cup, plastic bowl, and a two-liter soda bottle. Before the lesson, pour one cup of colored water into each container. (Use a drop or two of food coloring, but be careful—if it gets on clothing, it could stain.)

Display the containers and allow students time to examine them. Give each student a copy of the "Containers of Water" page. Ask students to color each picture to show the level of water in each container. Ask students to decide which containers have more, less, or the same amount of water. Number the pictures from 1 to 4, with 1 being the container they think has the least amount of water. When they finish, ask volunteers to measure the water in each container. Discuss the results with the class.

Measuring Tips

To prevent students from overfilling a container, mark the desired level on it with a felt pen or a thin piece of masking tape. Provide funnels if students need to fill containers with narrow openings.

How Much Will It Hold?

Gather up several clear containers with different shapes, such as a tall pitcher, a narrow-necked bottle (like the one that hold salad dressing), a wide bowl, a tea cup, a flat cake pan, a round pie pan, and a relish jar. Label the containers *A, B, C, D*, etc., and mark a fill line on each one with a black marker.

Have students label a page *A, B, C, D*, etc., and estimate how many cups of water will be needed to fill each container to the marked level.

Let students take turns filling containers with water from a measuring cup and announcing the results. Have students record the measurements next to their estimates. Discuss the results with the class. Ask students whether the shape of the containers influenced their ability to judge its capacity.

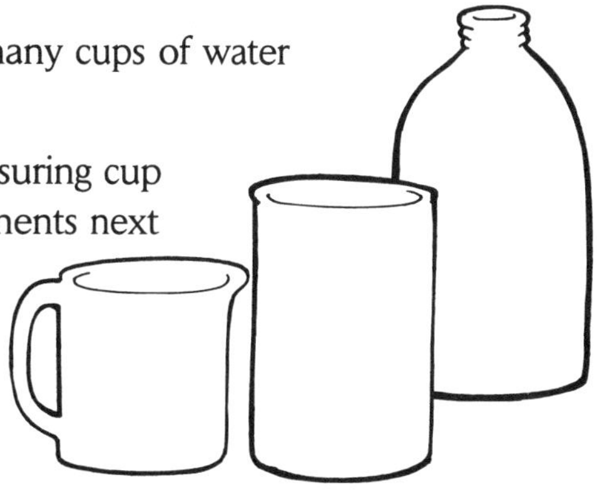

Name ________________________________ Date ______________

Containers of Water

Observe the water level in the four containers provided by your teacher.

Color the pictures to show the water level.

Number the pictures from 1 to 4 from least to most. The container marked number 1 would be the one you think has the least water.

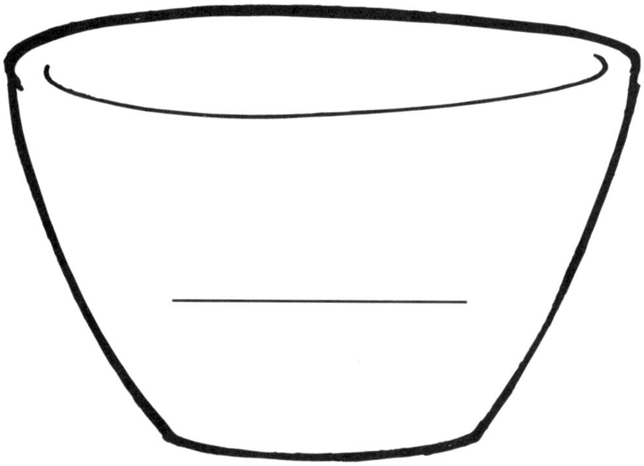

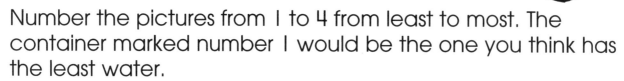

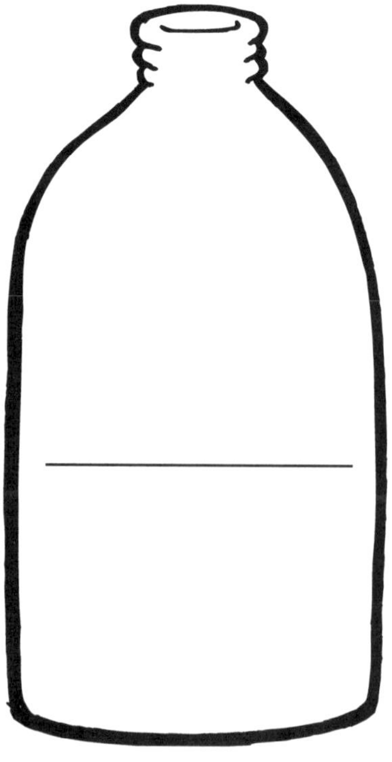

Estimating and Measuring Volume

Fill and Cover

Use Andrea Butler's book *Mr. Sun and Mr. Sea* as inspiration for this measuring activity. In this African legend, Mr. Sun flees to the sky when Mr. Sea's visits cover his home with a great expanse of water.

After reading the story, place a large rock in a deep plastic tub. Tell the class to imagine that the rock is Mr. Sun's house. Next, hold up a quart container and ask the class to estimate how many quarts it would take to cover the "house." Write their estimates on the board. Call on one student at a time to fill the quart container with water and empty it into the tub. Keep track of the number of quarts added to the tub. Stop when the rock is completely covered. Finally, have the class check the board to see who made the closest estimate.

Absorb the Spills

Cover a table with newspaper, paper towels, or cloth towels to absorb the spills. If you have a sink in the classroom, use the counter or nearby table for liquid measuring activities, so students will have easy access to water.

If your classroom has no sink, bring in a large plastic tub of water and set it on a table for students to use during measuring activities. If the weather is nice, set the tub of water on a table on the playground, where spills won't matter.

Fill the Jar

Ask parents to donate baby food jars and large mayonnaise jars for this measuring activity. You will need half as many jars as you have students.

Pair up students and give each pair a large jar and a small jar. Have students guess how many jars of water they will need to fill the big jar. Have students write their estimates on a sheet of paper. After they measure the capacity of the large jar with the small jar, they should record the actual measurement and compare it to their estimates.

Extension:

Have students estimate and then measure the capacity of the small jar by emptying tablespoons of water into it. Have them predict how many tablespoons of water they would need to fill the larger jar and then measure to check their estimates.

Pick a Button

Show the class two red buttons and two blue buttons before placing them in a paper bag. Ask students to predict which color is most likely to appear if they take out a button without looking. Have them explain their predictions. Call on a student to draw a button from the bag. Record the color on the board. Return the button to the bag, shake the bag, and repeat the activity ten times. Discuss the results.

Ask students how the chances of picking a red button could be increased without changing the number of buttons. (Use three red buttons and one blue one.) Help students check their predictions by changing the number of red buttons, drawing one at a time, and recording the results. Discuss the results. (By increasing the number of red buttons, the chances of picking a red button increased.)

Not Simply a Guess

Some students may think that predicting is simply another word for guessing. Tell the class that a prediction is an "educated guess." To make a prediction, they need to look at information and determine what is most likely to happen.

Penny Toss

Give each student a copy of "Penny Toss," a penny, and a place mat. (If you don't have place mats for cushioning the noise, use felt squares or towels.) Instruct students to shake the penny in their hands, toss it in the air, and let it land on the place mat. Have each student record the results. Discuss the results when they finish.

Spinner Game

Divide the class into groups of three and give each group a copy of the "Spinner Game," glue, thick cardboard, a sharp pencil, and a paper clip. Students should cut out the spinners and color them, then glue them to thick cardboard. A sharp pencil poked into the center of the circle allows them to use a paper clip as a spinner.

Have students predict on which spinner(s) the paper clip is most likely to land on red and on which spinner(s) the paper clip is least likely to land on red. (The paper clip is most likely to land on red with the circle that is $3/4$ red and least likely to land on red with the circle that has the smallest portion of it colored red.)

Have them spin ten times on each circle and keep a tally of the results. Display the results. Encourage students to compare their results with the results found by other groups.

Name ______________________ Date __________

Penny Toss

A penny has two sides. If you shake it in your hands and toss it in the air, it can land heads up or tails up.

heads **tails**

What do you think would happen if you tossed a penny 10 times?

☐ It will land heads up most of the time.

☐ It will land tails up most of the time.

☐ It will land heads up and tails up about the same number of times.

Try it. Toss the penny 10 times.

Write **h** for heads or **t** for tails to show how it lands.

1. ______ 5. ______ 9. ______
2. ______ 6. ______ 10. ______
3. ______ 7. ______
4. ______ 8. ______

How many times did your penny land heads up? ______

Tails up? ______

Compare your results with a classmate's.

What did you find out?

____

____

Name ______________________________ Date ______________

Spinner Game

Color the sections of the spinners red for **r** and yellow for **y**. Cut them out and glue to cardboard. Place one end of a paper clip in the center of the circle. Put a pencil point through the paper clip on the dot in the center. Then spin the paper clip.

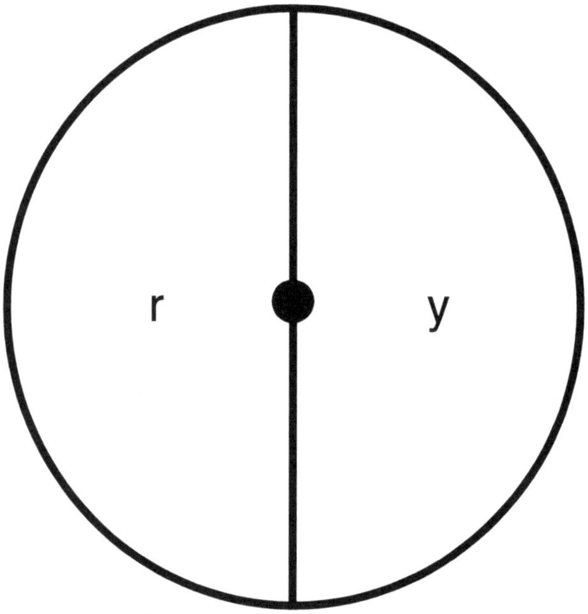

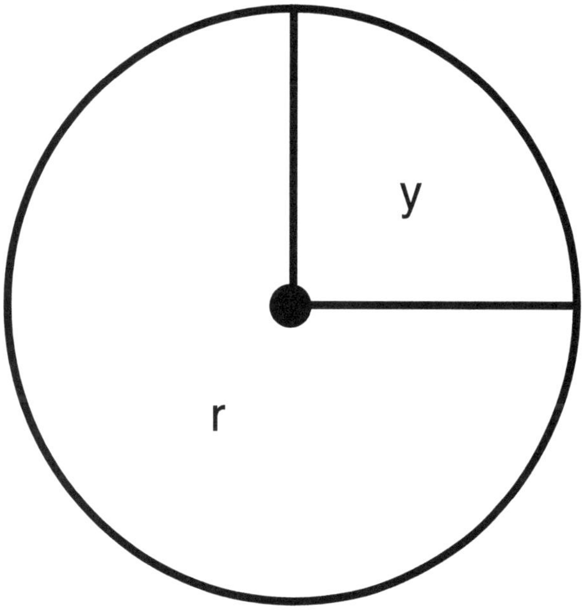

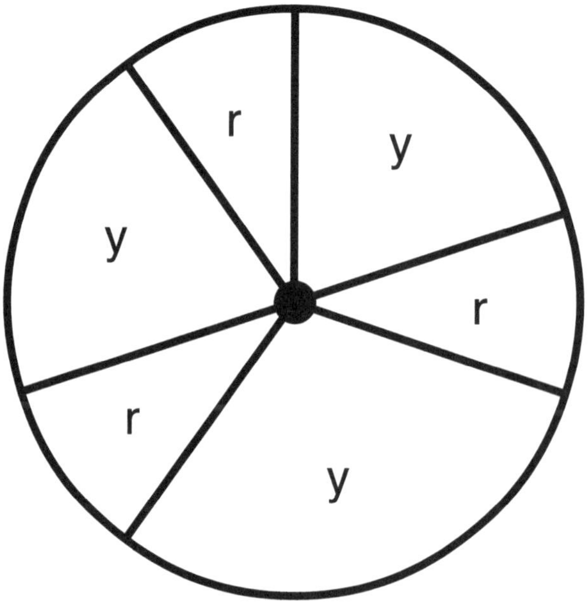

0-7682-2912-X *Fast Ideas for Busy Teachers: Math*

Multiplication

Multiplication Ants

Read *One Hundred Hungry Ants,* by Elinor Pincez, to the class. In the story, 100 ants march to a picnic in different formations: one row of 100, two rows of 50, four rows of 25, and so on. After reading the story, write *100* on a sheet of chart paper. Discuss the different ways the ants grouped themselves and have students help you write the corresponding multiplication facts on the board (1 x 100 = 100; 2 x 50 = 100).

Follow-Up Activity: Give each student a copy of "Marching Ants." Have them color the ants to show the multiplication facts you name. For 2 x 6, they would color two rows of six ants. After coloring the ants, students should outline the border with a marker or dark crayon to show the rectangle formed. Continue with several more multiplication facts, then ask students to cut out their rectangles, glue them onto white paper, and write the corresponding multiplication equations below.

Egg Carton Multiplication

Egg cartons provide a quick way for students to make equal groups of objects. After students fill the cups with small counters, they can write corresponding multiplication facts. For example, students who fill their cups with three counters each can see easily that 1 x 3 = 3, 2 x 3 = 6, and so on.

Addition and Multiplication

Ask six students to stand in front of the class. Arrange them in three groups of two. Have the class state a corresponding addition sentence (2 + 2 + 2 = 6) and write it on the board. Next, point out that there are an equal number of students in each group. Write *3 groups of 2* on the board. Tell students that when equal groups are added repeatedly, they can use multiplication to get the same results. Write *3 x 2 = 6* on the board.

Next, call eight students to the front of the room. Arrange them in four groups of two. Ask the rest of the class to state the corresponding addition and multiplication sentences. Repeat the activity with different students (or manipulatives) and other multiplication facts.

Tell the class that some numbers can be grouped in several ways. Call on 12 students to go to the front of the room. Ask the class for suggestions on different groupings (three rows of 4; two rows of 6; four rows of 3), and have the 12 students arrange themselves accordingly. Each time, write the corresponding multiplication fact on the board.

Marching Ants